SELF-CARE FOR BLACK WOMEN

OVERCOME SELF-SABOTAGE, BOOST CONFIDENCE,
AND CELEBRATE WHO YOU NATURALLY ARE

HOUSE OF ABUNDANCE PUBLICATIONS

CONTENTS

INTRODUCTION

"Anything you don't know is going to be hard at first, but if you stay the course, put the time and effort in, it will become seamless eventually."

— JEANETTE EPPS

Strength has always been a defining characteristic for black women, but over time, I've come to see that the phrase "Being a strong black woman" is killing us softly. While strong women are not particular to any race or culture of people, the question of strength has always been more of a gender and race mandate than a personal choice for black women.

People easily criticize and celebrate our ability to survive the hardships of black life down through the ages. Many of us now think that suffering and self-sacrifice are the critical ingredients of a strong or "good" woman. We've had to be strong for our parents, men, kids, and communities.

Sadly, these experiences eat up our happiness from deep inside to the extent we fail to get directions to overcome that which is silently killing our inner lives. When I began to look and listen to the black women I come across nowadays, it became clear that, while many of them have a lot to offer the world, they were not "getting theirs" in return.

For instance, the COVID-19 pandemic made life more difficult for black women in the workforce. According to a healthcare job report by HealthCareDive in 2022, black women were more widely represented in healthcare than any other demographic group; 36% of female healthcare aids were black.

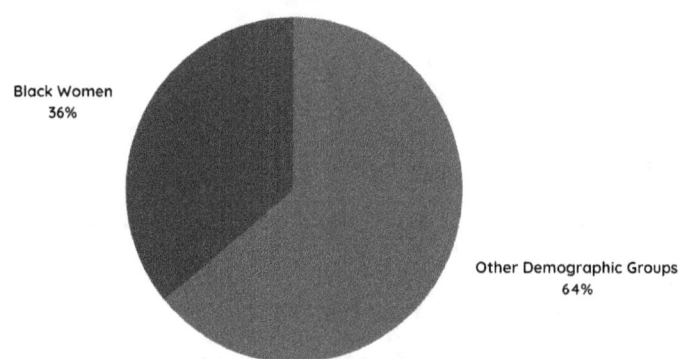

Black Women
36%

Other Demographic Groups
64%

Females in Healthcare Aid in the U.S

Meanwhile, this is one of the lowest-paid demographic, with the risks of no insurance, no paid sick leave, and a higher chance of catching COVID. Add this to more significant difficulties surrounding childcare. It has forced many black women to give up work.

It's like that almost every time. You experience a roller coaster ride of life traumas that causes prolonged stress that zaps your energy levels, causing physical and mental fatigue. In turn, it negatively affects your mood.

But why are you routinely effective in attending to everyone else's needs yet often fail to attend to your personal needs for recognition, respect, love, and gratitude?

What if you could have that same energy and power that the likes of Tina Turner have, despite all they have had to overcome.

Of course, this isn't the first time you're looking for a proven way to create the life you deserve, boost your confidence, and find ultimate happiness, is it?

So, why haven't you found a way yet?

When you read this book to the end, you'll discover how to:

- Peel back all the negativity that you have been carrying around
- Work on any healing and reframing your way of thinking so that self-care, self-love, and confidence becomes a natural part of your life
- Most importantly, live a happy life.

Many of you are probably asking yourselves, "Who are you to ask us to discover fulfillment in our lives, and why should we listen to you?"

That is a fair question, and I'd like to answer it at the outset of this book so that any doubts or reservations you may have about our own life experiences, qualifications, and intentions for this book are satisfied.

You see, we are a group of diverse, like-minded people determined to provide people with the resources and guidance they need to navigate today's turbulent waters. Together, we've experienced a wide range of horrible discrimination, not just because of skin color. This has caused many mental and physical health problems, including social anxiety, insomnia, eating disorders, high blood pressure, and everything in between.

So this isn't a book written by another well-meaning sister or someone who has no clue what it is like to be like you. What we want to share with you is too important to miss, so I hope you'll trust us to tell our story with candor, love, responsibility, respect, and integrity, starting with one of ours.

My name is Jayla Hogan, and I want you to take a journey with me to another side of yourself—a side beyond the educational degrees, achievements, titles, and material possessions. I want to speak candidly with you about you and me.

The build-up of stress from the COVID-19 pandemic was insane and overwhelming for most people I know and me. But of all of us struggling to avoid a mental breakdown, I can't think of anyone who suffered like my friend Sarah. Sarah lacked confidence and motivation during the pandemic; it took all her energy to get through the day. Her financial life was a mess; she had no personal freedom and lost her passion for pursuing her life goals and ambitions. All these drove her into anxiety and depression to the extent that she would get angry over the slightest issue.

You see, life was a great experience for Sarah until she lost her husband to a brief illness in late 2017, leaving her to take care of her two kids alone. Sarah worked as a midwife but couldn't keep a job with such uncertain hours as a single mother. By the fall season of 2019, Sarah had found a daytime shift as a waitress at a small restaurant in downtown Philadelphia. So she put her daughter in a creche and her son in daycare near her home in Fairmount.

Sarah would arrange playdates on weekends with her friends and their kids. Two years after losing her husband, she and her kids were beginning to feel less lonely, and their lives were starting to get back on track.

Sarah had been using her husband's life insurance to cover her rent and expenses all those times, but she blew through it not too long. So she had been catering to all the daily expenses while also trying to save some money.

Then, due to the COVID-19 pandemic, the restaurant, schools, and daycares all closed. No more playdates. Basic tasks that were usually more complicated when alone with a young child —shopping for food, dropping off laundry—suddenly got nerve-racking. And since nobody else could care for her children, she had no choice but to give up her work.

The months ahead became terrifying as Sarah had to use the little savings she had left. During the pandemic, it could take a week or more to get a grocery delivery slot in Philadelphia, and even when she did, she wouldn't have enough cash to pay for them. So she and her kids always ran out of food and personal items early.

As if that wasn't bad enough, Sarah felt isolated and insecure because of the discrimination against black people. Honestly, being a single black mom is lonely, even when there isn't any social distancing. The support system Sarah had put in place to keep her and her kids going had completely fallen apart.

Even when she found a job to do later on and her kids were back at school, things weren't the way they were anymore. All of the events and experiences had taken a toll on her. It wasn't until she sat back and broke down all that had happened to her that she discovered the only way she could see a change and a light at the end of the tunnel was to take care of herself.

While Sarah was tired of the whole situation, she knew she deserved better. She wanted a good life for herself and her children; she wanted to set the best example and build a legacy for them. Overall, she wanted to be an example to all.

During this period, I watched Sarah take the first step to making a change by embracing her color and celebrating her life. Afterward, she researched and spent time consulting life coaches, attending workshops, and purchasing self-help and self-care books.

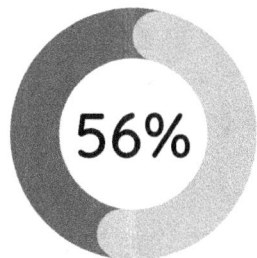

Adult Americans Opinions on Donald Trump & Racism (did he make racism worse?)

It wasn't easy as this happened to be a time 56% of adult Americans felt that Donald Trump had made racism worse. Every time Sarah found that drive to push herself out of the shadows of being a black woman, she encountered challenges she couldn't overcome, which only demoralized her more.

I may not have experienced exactly what Sarah went through, but I've had my fair share of struggles. However, the quote stated at the start of this introduction greatly helped me pull through. Jennette Epps made history as the first African-American woman to crew the International Space Station (ISS). She was also the second female to participate in CAVES, a training program for exploring unknown terrains such as those found on the Moon and Mars.

Over time, my friend Sarah realized that life shouldn't be a constant fight. This was after she discovered that it wasn't her fault that things had gotten worse and her personal life had gone downhill. If anything was to blame, it was all the misinformation out there. There are so many resources for women's self-care, but only a few are aimed at helping black women. The majority focus on issues like racism, gender pay gap, etc., rather than the how-to of self-care, and they aren't written from the perspective of a black woman.

When Sarah finally realized the issue, she turned to me for assistance. And so, I did intense research and followed up with what other great black women who challenged the status quo did. In the end, we came up with a solution that solved what would have taken Sarah several years to fix in less than a year. Finally, in 2021, Sarah got her life back on track after a few more trials. Her career took a new turn, and she became happy, affirmed, and fulfilled. She healed from her past, got a happy home, and was able to pursue her lifelong goals.

Today, there are many black women like Sarah, whose experiences may be different, yet they were able to break barriers and accomplish a remarkable feat just by using the secrets you will discover in this book. Phenomenal black women like Michelle Obama, Sydney Barber, Stacey Abrams, and many others have played a key role in advancing American society in every area, from politics to sports to service industries.

So we came together at House of Abundance Publications and agreed to share our struggles to enable us to overcome any shame or guilt we felt and support each other in finding a way through our problems. After years of research and experience, we want to share our knowledge and help people like you.

Self-Care for Black Women will help you take charge of your power. It will move you further in the direction of your self-realization and happiness and help you cultivate healthy self-care habits. While writing this guide, we conducted about twenty face-to-face one-hour interviews with different black women to gain a deeper understanding of the issues they were facing in their lives.

We collected data from hundreds of black women and men using long focus-group sessions and hour-long one-on-one interviews, by phone or in person, over six months from late 2021 to the 2nd quarter of 2022. So you see—it took us more than eight months to create this guide, and it cost us a lot of time, money, and resources, but it was worth it. So I hope this book will inspire you to make this profound shift toward greater joy in your life.

In the end, you'll be able to beat the broken system, heal from the past and learn how to change how you view yourself to overcome self-sabotage, discover your coping skills, and find true happiness. It'll help you become flexible with your time and freedom; have more time for yourself, family, and friends, and live a better lifestyle. Trust me—you don't want to be left out. We put together this roadmap to help you discover that self-care is the ultimate form of protest. Prioritizing and loving yourself is the key to ultimate happiness. Feeling excited already?

Well, then, let's get started!

1

SETTING THE MISCONCEPTIONS OF SELF-CARE STRAIGHT

"Self-care is how you take your power back."

— LALAH DELIA

One evening, Chloe sat by the window in her room, gazing at the sunset while feeling awash with many thoughts and emotions. She had returned to work four weeks after giving birth to Jayla. And four and a half years ago, when she gave birth to her twin sons, she returned to work after just six weeks. In both cases, her husband had encouraged her to take enough time off work for the family; he was indeed her biggest champion. However, Chloe was anxious about all the time she would lose at work if she spent too long at home.

She didn't need to return to work so soon. After all, the *Daily Mail Group* and *HuffPost*, the media outlets where she worked, had regular maternity leave policies. Still, she rushed back to work twice, after C-sections and while nursing. Chloe hated every minute of work in those early months. She was constantly in a state of conflict, wishing she was home while at work.

She would be worried about cleaning the home, doing the laundry, ironing the clothes, and filling up the cupboards. She felt an intense need to protect and provide for her three children, home, and parents, who relied on her. At the same time, she wanted to protect her full-time jobs at both news outlets. Chloe was highly driven to succeed in her career, and she felt that since she worked for media agencies, she somehow needed to be present to succeed.

All those times, Chloe would convince herself she was ultimately doing the right thing for her family, relationships, and career. Her idea of self-care was doing household chores and ensuring everyone was okay, but she was unconsciously putting too much pressure on herself.

Over time, she got overwhelmed by her family's dependence on her. She wondered if she was doing things right and was dizzy from the many emotions she never knew she could feel all at once.

She realized she had stopped caring for herself; she no longer had time to meditate or have bubble baths with scented candles and a glass of wine. She sorely missed those days she had romantic, relaxing aromatherapy. This overwhelming feeling continued until she was driven into a deep state of worry, anxiety, and, eventually, depression. But rather than seek help,

Chloe suffered in silence, thinking her problems weren't important enough to bother anyone with them.

While I sat and listened to Chloe as she shared her story with me, I realized that self-care was not something taught or promoted in society. It was something we had to learn ourselves.

You see, the importance of self-care cannot be overemphasized. Practicing self-care can lessen or altogether remove your anxiety, despair, and stress and boost your happiness, energy, and focus. So I want us to start by looking into the importance of self-care, especially for black women. You will learn what self-care is and isn't, and better understand the different areas of self-care.

SELF-CARE IS CRUCIAL FOR EVERYONE, BUT WHY IS IT MORE IMPORTANT FOR BLACK WOMEN?

What comes to mind when you hear the word "self-care"? Pedicures? Maybe facials? All these are great, but in the end, they are simply physical care. And while physical self-care is a significant aspect of the bigger picture, there are other essential aspects of self-care. This can include things like letting go of overthinking and perfectionism, hiring a babysitter so that you can rest or go on a date, saying no to stressful activities, declining to do things out of guilt, and allowing yourself much-needed rest and downtime to refuel.

To live, love, and fulfill your responsibilities as a parent, you must take care of yourself in all aspects—emotionally, cognitively, physically, socially, spiritually, practically, and professionally. This is self-care.

The COVID-19 pandemic must have taught you the value of caring for yourself when faced with stress, uncertainty, and worry. For black women, who often face an excessive burden in society, you can use self-care to counter the trauma of dealing with racism and stress in the home and workplace. More than any other previous event, the pandemic highlighted that self-care can occasionally be an efficient form of community care.

Take the U.S., for instance. The nation is under more stress now than in recent decades. "Stress in America: The State of Our Nation," a 2017 report by the American Psychological Association (APA), reported that 63% of Americans worry about the country's future, 62% worry about money, and 61% worry about their jobs.

After the 2016 election, tensions surrounding these topics skyrocketed, then grew during the 2020 pandemic before erupting during widespread agitation with the Black Lives Matter movement's urgent call for social justice. Unsurprisingly, the APA poll also found that racial and gender injustices enhanced social anxiety.

Political tension, social movements, and the pandemic have all highlighted the struggles unique to black women, including racism, classism, sexism, heterosexism, and anti-transgender violence. Black women are often the caregivers and play a role in the community, which adds to the stress. Furthermore, there is this image and expectation that black women are strong and that we can handle anything (I talked about this in the intro-duction).

Our resilience has been transformed into a galvanized layer of armor that protects us from suffering while robbing us of a natural and fulfilling existence. Despite all we have accom-plished, everyone around us—friends, family, and coworkers—has decided that we have become too hard, too aloof, too inde-pendent, and too strong.

As I listened to Chloe, I saw how frustrated she was feeling. Exhausted from staying up until 2 a.m. the previous night to do laundry, she had been beating herself up all day about not deliv-ering a handmade supper to her neighbor, who had recently lost her mother. She had also skipped breakfast and lunch a few times. I was so sorry for her. Most of us would never allow our kids to go without food or sleep; we would never ignore their physical or emotional needs.

But as mothers, we subject ourselves to this regularly. It's diffi-cult and lonely to live as a strong black woman who must always be on her own as a caregiver, survivor, and provider. And as we all know, wearing armor day and night significantly adds to this weight. This "strong black woman" lifestyle might eventually and severely hurt your mental and physical health.

We should provide the same kind of love, tender care, and compassion that we freely give our children and family. We should teach our children about self-worth and respecting one's values through our deeds rather than words.

Modeling self-love and self-care is the most effective way to positively impact your self-esteem and how you view yourself. This is what self-care is all about. You have to decide to put your well-being before that of others. This decision shows the world we recognize and appreciate our self-worth and value.

7 POPULAR MISCONCEPTIONS OF SELF-CARE

During the years I have talked to some women about self-care, I have noticed some black women's achievements start to trump their fulfillment. So many of these highly successful black women have realized the American Dream. They have substituted ambition for love, relationships, and family to the point that there are disturbing misconceptions about what self-care even means. Some see self-care as simply doing their favorite things or as something optional.

I knew this issue deserves a more profound study, so I explored six popular misconceptions of self-care so you can bust them and make happiness, fulfillment, and love part of your life again.

1. Self-care is selfish

Being selfish means desiring to take from others, often to their detriment. But this isn't what self-care is; self-care is about replenishing your resources without depleting someone else's.

I understand that you feel people might think of you as a terrible person when you refuse to help them to your detriment, but rest assured that will not stop them from trying to convince you of the exact opposite. Although it is typical for people to feel excluded or abandoned in such situations, understand that it is in your best interest to avoid overextending yourself.

Self-care is a way to recharge your energy and promote overall well-being (as discussed in the next section). You are setting an excellent example for others by doing this for yourself. One of the healthiest things you can do for yourself and everyone else is to be aware of your emotional health and embrace your feelings.

2. It is all about doing things that make you happy

Self-care is not just about doing things that make you happy; it is also a moment to spoil yourself with luxury. Although self-care may sometimes involve these things, this is a huge over-simplification of the concept.

Daily self-care practices will vary because they can take many forms and have many distinct functions. In an ideal world, you would assess your requirements at every given time and adjust your self-care accordingly.

As a result, sometimes, you may need to do one of your favorite things, while other times, you may need to find the drive to complete an ignored activity that is still causing you tension. You will have a wide range of practices at your disposal that you may use to customize to your needs when practiced optimally.

3. You need to make a significant financial investment to do self-care

As the self-care trend gained traction, many businesses, particularly wellness businesses, jumped on the self-care bandwagon to develop, market, and sell self-care goods and services, including bath bombs, yoga mats, candles, and skincare products.

You can easily practice self-care without buying these things; simply check your home for alternatives. I have some of my own favorite product-free self-care techniques. While money does not directly contribute to greater happiness, it is a stress-relieving buffer.

Self-care is difficult when you don't have enough money to meet your fundamental necessities. Permitting myself to make mistakes occasionally is one of the most acceptable ways I can practice self-care because I have always been a perfectionist. The fun part is that no money is involved in this self-care practice!

4. Self-care requires a lot of time

Many believe self-care requires a lot of time because it has been connected with activities like getting a massage or following a 15-step skincare regimen. Like the previous misconception, engaging in time-consuming hobbies may benefit certain people, but it is unnecessary. There are ways to practice self-care while attending to daily, time-consuming demands. When you feel pressured, for instance, you could pause and take deep breaths, eat nourishing meals, take a break from your devices, or engage in thankfulness exercises. None of these activities take much time, and even little self-care breaks can improve composure, mental clarity, and enjoyment.

On the other hand, if what you need takes too much time, you can fit it into your weekly schedule. If you tend to put others' demands ahead of your own, setting your own needs and scheduling other commitments around it may be just what you need (though I realize not everyone can do this).

5. Self-care should not be a priority

Self-care may not always be a top priority in your life, but it is the first thing to suffer when things get hectic. If there is a lot of pressure to finish a task, you will feel bad for doing something else. Thus, self-care is most necessary when you're stressed out or feeling overworked.

Practicing self-care often provides us with additional vigor and drive to finish those activities. When we regard self-care as a regular and necessary preventive action (like brushing your teeth), the effects on our wellness are remarkable and long-lasting.

6. Self-care is only for women

That is largely untrue. Self-care is not exclusively reserved for women. Self-care is an essential practice that everyone, regardless of their gender, should prioritize in their daily lives. It is a way of caring for your physical, emotional, and mental well-being and is crucial for maintaining a healthy and balanced life-style. Self-care is not just for women; it is for everyone who wants to live a happier and healthier life. Self-care activities, such as meditation, exercise, getting enough sleep, and eating healthy, can help reduce stress, boost mood, and improve overall health. It's important to remember that taking care of yourself is not selfish but rather an act of self-love and self-respect.

Self-care equips us with the tools we need to reform ourselves, which in turn helps us improve our minds and help everyone. Additionally, practicing self-care can help you build resilience, improve your relationships, and enhance your productivity. It's important to remember that self-care isn't selfish, but rather, it's necessary for living a happy and fulfilling life. So, I encourage you to prioritize self-care in your daily life and take care of yourself physically and mentally.

Anyone interested in learning more about self-care may find that projecting these uplifting nonverbal cues can shift the game. When the outside world throws things at you every five minutes, you cannot afford to back down and not put effort into improving yourself. You can't expect to succeed if you don't care for yourself. Therefore, it is untrue to say that self-care is solely for women.

7. Self-Care Does Not Affect How We Interact With Other People

One of the biggest myths about self-care is that it only affects individuals and does not impact our interactions with others.

However, this couldn't be further from the truth. Taking care of ourselves has a direct effect on how we interact with others, and this includes both verbal and nonverbal communication. When we prioritize self-care, we become more attuned to our needs, and as a result, we can communicate more effectively and empathetically with others. Additionally, nonverbal cues such as body language, tone of voice, and facial expressions play a crucial role in our communication with others. When we're stressed, tired, or run down, these nonverbal cues can be affected, leading to misunderstandings, misinterpretations, and even conflict. By prioritizing self-care, we can ensure that we're showing up as our best selves in our interactions with others, both verbally and nonverbally. So, I encourage you to take care of yourself, not just for your benefit but also for those around you.

THE 7 ASPECTS OF SELF-CARE

We usually assign priorities based on our needs. Rent must be paid, so you put financial self-care ahead of a job that generates income. Depending on your past experiences, you might need to take precautions to ensure that you feel secure in social situations. For example, you might choose to attend an online hangout but decline an in-person invitation. That is also a form of self-care. While expanding your perspective on self-care, you may find significance in the less enjoyable aspects of your day and maintain a high priority for yourself.

Self-care involves much more than just filling your room with scented candles; it also involves taking care of your intellectual demands and valuing your social skills. Below are seven aspects of self-care you must know to begin nurturing yourself and making self-renewal part of your everyday life:

1. Emotional self-care

Thousands of black women have been emotionally abused, neglected, or smothered by their parents, other significant guardians, and loved ones. Many of these women do not realize they were used or neglected, so they continue to suffer from many problems throughout their lives because they are not getting the help they need.

People who internalize their abuse usually manifest self-destructiveness, depression, suicidal ideation, passivity, with-drawal and avoiding most types of social contact, shyness, and very little communication with others. They are also most likely to have low self-esteem as well as suffer from guilt, remorse, depression, loneliness, and rejection.

Emotional self-care allows us to regulate our emotions and cope with complicated feelings as they arise. By regularly engaging in emotional self-care, you will be able to connect with your feelings and healthily process them, as this is critical to your happiness and overall well-being.

Examples of emotional self-care activities include the following:

- Having a heart-to-heart with a close friend or mentor
- Thinking positively about yourself (try not to criticize yourself for one week!)
- Seeking support from a therapist, coach, social worker, or counselor
- Journaling—writing down your thoughts and feelings
- Going on a fun date alone, with your partner, or organizing a monthly girls' night out

Paying attention to how you speak to yourself is the best place to start when trying to take care of your emotional well-being. A crucial first step in overcoming a bad habit is recognizing when you are talking negatively to yourself. The next stage is affirming kind words every day instead of critical remarks.

2. Mental self-care

The mental aspect of self-care is the basis for other aspects and often has a physical cause. It begins when psychological or emotional stress (such as the loss of a loved one) triggers chemical imbalances in the brain. While some of us can withstand more stress than others, nobody is immune to issues associated with mental health.

Therefore, you must understand and develop a loving relationship with your mind; you do not necessarily have to reach a mental state of nirvana! Mental self-care involves you stimulating your mind and cultivating a healthy psyche.

Examples of mental self-care activities include the following:

- Reading a good book or seeing an intellectually stimulating movie
- Learning a new skill or hobby
- Signing up for a class or workshop on a topic that interests you
- Challenging yourself to learn something new in your community or at work

Ideally, you want to learn how to control your thoughts, set clear boundaries with friends, family, and work, and know when it is right to consult a professional for help. You also want to incorporate the above mental safe-care activities into your everyday life.

3. Physical self-care

Undoubtedly, physical self-care is one popular aspect of self-care most of us think of whenever it comes to caring for ourselves. It usually involves activities you deliberately engage in to enhance your physical well-being.

Everyone should take care of their physical health, but your choice will depend on your lifestyle. Take your dog for a walk as self-care if you spend the day in an office chair. On the other hand, if you work all day in construction, you might want to practice restorative yoga at the end of your shift.

Examples of physical self-care activities include the following:

- Being kind and loving to your body—appreciate your body
- Nourish your body by eating healthy and nutritious foods that make you feel amazing
- Eating extra fruit and veggies to keep your body fresh and strengthen your immune system
- Getting enough sleep and staying hydrated by drinking enough water
- Exercising to replenish your energy and manage stress
- Taking the time to enjoy, nurture, and appreciate your physical appearance

Other physical self-care tasks include going to the doctor when ill and taking time off to relax properly. You could also hike, take a yoga class, play a sport you like, or go on a walk. Just don't forget to strike a balance! Being busy is inevitable, but you should always relax when your body requests it.

4. Social self-care

Socialization and close relationships with people are other essential aspects of our well-being. Your relationships give you people who will listen to you, support you, and create memories with you.

It may be harder now than usual to maintain your friendships as a part of social self-care because of certain issues you are experiencing. However, there are still ways to save those struggling relationships. Believe it or not—your welfare partly depends on having a supportive social network.

Examples of social self-care activities include:

- Prioritizing your relationships with people and setting boundaries
- Reaching out to others and building relationships that recharge you (this will add meaning to your life and make you feel fulfilled)
- Focusing on quality time while having meaningful, interactive conversations and doing fun things with close friends.

5. Spiritual self-care

Everyone may benefit from this type of self-care regardless of their beliefs. Any activity that feeds your soul and spirit, and makes you think beyond yourself, is considered spiritual self-care.

Even though spiritual self-care is a religious activity for some people, it doesn't necessarily have to be that way for you. Fundamentally, this technique is about connecting with your inner spirit. Some people often do activities that involve honoring a belief in a higher power—this higher power could be God, the universe, or something else.

Everyone can benefit from practicing spiritual self-care, especially if they want to feel more rooted in their daily lives. It can offer solace to people experiencing loss and grief, uncertainty in their health or finances, or any other challenging life circumstances.

Examples of spiritual self-care activities include:

- Taking some alone time to write about or reflect on your feelings
- Taking a walk in a park or the woods
- Fellowshipping with people of your faith
- Meditating, praying, and reflecting on what you are grateful for
- Doing something creative, like painting, drawing, writing, dancing, and singing
- Volunteering for a cause you are passionate about

When doing spiritual self-care, try implementing a daily spiritual practice into your routine and pick a calm, private spot in your house. Avoid opening social media first thing in the morning. Instead, start your day with mantras that uplift your soul to ensure success.

6. Practical self-care

Practical self-care is carrying out tasks that satisfy fundamental parts of your life to avert unpleasant situations in the future. Even if these self-care activities are less fun than others, they are no less essential and can make you feel considerably better. For example, consider how much better you feel when you keep up with your workout schedule.

Practicing practical self-care can help us feel more in control and at peace in our hectic lives. Practical self-care may be just what you need if you're still in college, a young professional, a caretaker, a stay-at-home mom, or someone who has trouble staying organized.

Examples of practical self-care activities include:

- Organizing your living space or workspace
- Creating sustainable healthy habits
- Planning your finances and investing right
- Doing the laundry for the week in advance

You can also use practical self-care to commit to a better sleep schedule, declutter your bedroom, take professional development classes, and much more.

7. Professional self-care

Self-care is essential for more than just your personal life. It is equally vital for your professional and business lives. For instance, working from home and avoiding social interaction might affect our well-being.

Practicing professional self-care and learning to arm yourself with new tools is crucial to better manage stress and perform successfully. Even if you enjoy your work and don't find it incredibly demanding, maintaining a professional self-care routine can help you avoid burnout and keep your motivation.

Examples of professional self-care activities include:

- Taking courses and attending conferences related to your job
- Working with a mentor to build your skills and support your career
- Having a good relationship with coworkers after work hours
- Putting your phone on "Do Not Disturb" to avoid unnecessary calls
- Taking leave or going on vacation when necessary

Once you achieve a better work-life balance, you may find that there is more time to focus on the other six areas of self-care we have covered.

Despite all the crazy experiences that drove me into anxiety and depression due to the accumulated stress from the COVID-19 pandemic, I managed to emerge from my past pains and disappointments. I rediscovered and redefined my life in my late thirties, and so can you.

Suppose I could find the courage to resolve that. In that case, I will not give in to feeling sorry for myself, depression, or health challenges, and if I can move past the belief that I cannot be happy because I didn't check off every item on the list everyone told me I had to complete by the time I was thirty-five, so can you.

If I can make a change by embracing my color, celebrating my life, pursuing the passion of my dreams, and finding myself just a few years later, living the exact life I always wanted, so can you.

You see, sisters, for too long, we have allowed ourselves to be defined by other people's perceptions of who we are and how we should act and feel. That has got to change because these perceptions aren't us and have never been us. This book is for every black woman. I have spent the past three years traveling around the country, talking with, listening to, working with, and supporting many black women. I have been deeply touched by all our triumphs and tragedies during this time.

SELF-CARE ASSESSMENT EXERCISE

As we round off this chapter, here is a simple exercise for you. This exercise is not exhaustive, it is merely suggestive. So feel free to modify whatever areas that are relevant for you.

Step 1

I want you to think about your self-care behaviors—the emotional, mental, physical, social, spiritual, practical, and professional— over the past 30 days.

Step 2

Take the time to reflect on how you feel and identify your good and destructive emotions. Write down these behaviors in separate columns.

Step 3

Using your answers above, check to see if there are items on the list that make you think, "Could I really do this?" It could be anger, fear, shame, anxiety, or sadness. Take particular note of these things you would like to change in your life.

Step 4

Now look at the good emotions and look for patterns in your responses. Are you more or less active in some areas of self-care than others? Listen to your inner voice and note anything you want to improve or feel you must prioritize over the next 30 days.

For example, you may write statements like the ones below:

- I will focus on the things I can control
- I will create time for personal reflection
- I will take a break from social media (try to specify how much time off social media you will take)
- I will attend a counseling/therapy session
- I will ask for help when I need it
- I challenge my negative thoughts
- I will set boundaries in my relationships
- I will avoid situations that will trigger bad memories or emotions

Going forward, we will be taking a deep dive into the mental self-care aspect. Of the seven aspects of self-care, mental self-care is the cure to unraveling the other aspects. There is such a strong link between mental and physical health that we will start with what is going on in your mind, even so far buried that you are unaware it is there.

KEY POINTS

- Practicing self-care can lessen or altogether remove your anxiety, despair, and stress and boost your happiness, energy, and attention.
- To live, love, and fulfill your responsibilities as a parent, you must take care of yourself in all aspects—emotionally, cognitively, physically, socially, spiritually, practically, and professionally.
- Modeling self-love and self-care is the most effective way to positively impact your self-esteem and how you view yourself.
- Self-care is a way to recharge your energy, which promotes overall well-being.
- Self-care equips us with the tools we need to reform ourselves, which in turn helps us improve our minds and help everyone.
- Self-care involves much more than just filling your room with scented candles; it also involves taking care of your intellectual demands and valuing your social skills.

2

IT ALL STARTS WITH YOUR MENTAL WELL-BEING

"Nothing is worth diminishing your health. Nothing is worth poisoning yourself into stress, anxiety, and fear."

— STEVE MARABOLI

According to a report from Psychiatric Times, the prevalence of poor mental health was about 23.4% in women and 15.6% in men in 2017. In addition, the frequency of depression diagnoses was much higher in women, with 19.4% in women and only 8.5% in men. This shows that women suffer from depression twice as much as men.

Looking at these statistics, you may think that the percentage of black women receiving care is similar to that of white women. But the report further reveals that black women dealing with mental health challenges are only about half as likely to receive the care and support they need.

Remember my friend Sarah? Well, she shared her recent traumatic experience with me, and I think sharing it here will help you better understand the struggles people with depression face. Some months ago, Sarah visited a supermarket in Fairmount just as it was opening. She arrived early that morning because she wanted to avoid the crowd of shoppers she had met the previous afternoon.

Fortunately, Sarah was the first customer that day, and she felt calm as she grabbed a shopping cart and strolled toward the produce section. She was relieved that she didn't feel as self-conscious as she had felt the previous day. She was also glad that her kids hadn't noticed she was struggling with anxiety the day before, or else they might have thought she was crazy.

But just as Sarah reached the end of the aisle, the produce manager called out to someone and then disappeared into the storeroom. Suddenly, Sarah was all alone in the store. The long rows of canned goods made her head light, and she gasped for breath. Her knees felt weak, her hands turned cold and numb, and she began to tremble like her world was falling apart.

What struck Sarah most about these feelings was their intensity. They were fierce and overwhelming, even when nothing in the supermarket suggested that she was in imminent danger. At some point, Sarah began to wonder if she was slowly losing her mind.

Eventually, she abandoned her shopping cart and made for the entrance, struggling to keep her emotions in check. She headed straight to the emergency room at a nearby hospital, and after a doctor examined her, he told her she was experiencing panic attacks due to post-traumatic stress disorder (PTSD). Unfortunately, these panic attacks have been Sarah's reality since she lost her husband.

And it's not just Sarah who experiences these attacks. I have encountered many other black women who experience intense emotional reactions that follow a sudden, unexpected episode of PTSD. Panic attacks are manifestations of psychological stress, warning signals that remind us black women to care for ourselves.

Sadly, we black women still face significant disparities in mental health care. Many mental health professionals agree that black women are among the most oppressed group in America, frequently dealing with racism, misogyny, and economic injustice. Moreover, others contend that black women are among the most resilient people in the world for this same reason.

Therefore, we must carefully understand the state of our mental health and see how we can create awareness, reduce stigma against black women with mental illnesses, and improve access to healthcare. Our past has a way of sticking with us and significantly impacting how we view the world today. This may range from a difficult childhood to traumatic experiences that can be suppressed and cause issues in adulthood. However, in this chapter, we will look into these problems and see how they are linked to our physical health.

WHAT IS TRAUMA?

According to the American Psychological Association, trauma is "an emotional response to a terrible event, like an accident, rape, or natural disaster." Any traumatic events we experience, whether during our childhood or as adults, can leave a lasting impact on our lives. These occurrences are usually out of our control and could dictate our daily lives if we allow them. Trauma could stem from any of the following:

- Physical, sexual, and emotional abuse
- Childhood neglect or abandonment
- Any form of violence (like domestic or gun violence)
- Living with a family member or a friend with mental health struggles or substance abuse
- Sudden, unexpected separation from a loved one
- Acts of terrorism or war
- A pandemic
- Health conditions or childbirth issues

Trauma is the single most typical cause of death for black women under forty and the third most typical cause of death at all ages. In addition, trauma patients in emergency departments have the most complex and challenging problems. Evidence in the United States and Europe shows that such cases are frequently mismanaged, with increased mortality and morbidity resulting from delays, misdiagnosis, and mistreatment. And this is more likely because of the inequality we black women experience in the healthcare system.

I wrote this book because everyone seems to have misconceptions about strong, accomplished black women, and that's not very good. We can all agree that black American women have gotten a bad rap for too long, and this has taken a toll on our mental health in one way or another. Some of it, perhaps, we have earned, and we need to take responsibility for that. But most of it has no connection to the women we are.

Almost daily, a video making fun of us goes viral on the internet. I, for one, am tired of this, and it's high time we set the record straight. It is not that we do not have a sense of humor because we do. But the issue is that everyone has an opinion about who we are and what troubles us.

Our society portrays black women as vulnerable, uneducated, and oppressed. People see us as self-sacrificing matriarchs who would do anything to assure our family's survival or the sexless lady who is the pillar of the church and is always there for their siren sister—the tragic mulatto. These mindsets end up pushing us into developing anxiety, depression, and other mental issues.

Post-Traumatic Stress Disorder (PTSD)

It is a widely known fact that trauma has mental and physical consequences, which can linger or worsen in the days, weeks, or months following the traumatic event. When this happens, the result is usually PTSD, and this can severely hurt your daily life and relationships. Severe anxiety, flashbacks, and enduring memories of the traumatic event are some symptoms you might experience if you have PTSD.

The link between physical and mental health is generally accepted in that physical illnesses hurt our mental health, and mental illnesses aggravate or prolong physical problems. For example, you could experience PTSD due to your previous anxiety or depression, a deep wound, or some financial challenges you're dealing with. There is also a long history of recognition, at least anecdotally, that survivors may also suffer mental health difficulties, even if they have not sustained physical injury.

Childhood Trauma

According to research, children are also vulnerable to trauma because their brain is still developing, and the release of stress hormones can impact this development. Naturally, when children experience horrible things, their stress levels rise, and their bodies release hormones linked to anxiety and terror.

Such developmental stress can obstruct healthy brain growth. Thus, trauma can significantly impact a child's long-term emotional development, mental health, physical health, and behavior. This is especially true with chronic trauma.

Even as an adult, the feeling of helplessness and anxiety could linger, thereby increasing the person's risk of slipping into depression.

Racial Trauma

There is also racial trauma, caused by race-based traumatic stress (RBTS). It describes how you respond to mental and emotional hurt caused by gloomy race-related encounters—that is, systemic racism. For instance, an FBI report regarding crime in the United States reveals that despite making up over 33% of the prison population, black people make up about 12 % of the country's population. The criminal justice system's racial tactics in policing, making arrests, and sentencing are all reflected in this data.

We can see this in the case of George Floyd, who was murdered by Derek Chauvin, a white Minneapolis police officer. And this was because of use of excessive force by police officers against black suspects and the lack of police accountability. George Floyd's girlfriend, Courteney Ross, also suffered trauma from George's death. "I've never felt more isolated," Ross stated. "Everyone's got their own thing going because of Floyd; everyone's on this journey, and I still don't know what to do or feel." Ross's case shows that you do not need to have suffered racism firsthand to be traumatized.

Research has found that when you experience RBTS, you experience physical and emotional symptoms similar to PTSD. In other words, experiencing racial discrimination, prejudice, hate crimes, or microaggressions might cause PTSD.

This suggests that you might be going through a mild case of PTSD right now. For instance, PTSD manifests itself when you have paranoid or obsessional beliefs about how you should behave so that you are not perceived as a threat. As a result, your entire body's functioning is disrupted.

Dealing with stress is hard—that much is true. It causes more crippling illnesses. Additionally, racial tension is fatal. It results in diseases that kill your mind, body, and soul. When you have PTSD symptoms, you become too concerned with protecting yourself from the perceived threat. You find it challenging to take life as it comes. Unfortunately, nobody has time for that when all we're trying to do is get by as black women in a sexist and racist world.

Therefore, as black women, it is time we had candid and meaningful conversations about how far we have come and how far we still have to go in valuing the things that truly matter in life. We must work on releasing ourselves from the stereotypes, negative images, and narratives that misrepresent us, affect our mental health, and cause us trauma.

THE IMPACT OF POOR MENTAL HEALTH ON OUR PHYSICAL SELVES

When you experience stress, a series of mental processes begin. The amygdala, the part of the brain that manages fear-related emotions, first learns about the stressor from your senses. Then, the hypothalamus, the control center of your brain, receives a signal if it regards that information as threatening or hazardous.

The autonomic nervous system connects the hypothalamus to the rest of your body. Through two different systems—the sympathetic and parasympathetic—automatic processes like breathing and heartbeat are regulated.

The "fight, flight, or freeze" reaction is set off by the sympathetic nervous system, which gives you enough energy to respond to a threat. In contrast, the parasympathetic nervous system allows your body to enter a "rest and digest" mode to help you relax when things are safer.

Your sympathetic nervous system is activated, and your adrenal glands are signaled by your hypothalamus when it receives information from your amygdala that you are in danger. Then, your heart beats faster due to the adrenaline your adrenal glands release, forcing more blood into your muscles and organs.

Your senses may also become more acute, and your respiration may speed up. Additionally, your body will release sugar into your bloodstream, supplying all regions with energy.

The hypothalamus activates the hypothalamic-pituitary-adrenal (HPA) axis, which is a network of the hypothalamus, anterior pituitary gland, and adrenal gland. As a result, more stress hormones, such as cortisol, may be released in these areas, forcing your body to maintain a constant state of alertness and vigilance.

The sympathetic nervous system's chemical release during stress has both immediate and long-term consequences on nearly every other bodily system:

- **Musculoskeletal system:** When a stressor enters your body, your muscles stiffen up quickly before releasing it. Long-term consequences of constant muscle tension include chronic pain conditions, including tension headaches and migraines.

- **Respiratory system:** The immediate action makes you breathe more forcefully and quickly, and you may even hyperventilate, which can lead to panic attacks in some people. While inhaling hard can make it challenging to receive adequate oxygen, the long-term effect can be devastating if you have a respiratory condition such as asthma or emphysema.

- **Cardiovascular system:** Your heart will beat more quickly and vigorously, and your blood vessels will widen, allowing more blood to flow to your massive muscles and increasing your blood pressure. The usual long-term effects are consistently raised heart rate, blood pressure, and stress hormones, which might increase your risk of a heart attack, stroke, or hypertension. Additionally, these long-term effects may increase your cholesterol levels and irritate your cardiovascular system.

- **Endocrine system:** Adrenaline and cortisol, two stress hormones, offer your body the energy it needs to either fight or flee from a stressor in the short-term. Your liver also creates more blood sugar to provide your body with energy. The long-term effects of excessive cortisol include thyroid issues, cognitive impairment, and the development of belly fat. Additionally, some people may be more susceptible to type-2 diabetes because they don't reabsorb the additional blood sugar that their liver excretes.

Our menstrual cycle and the frequency of our periods can both be impacted by chronic stress. Additionally, they may interfere with conception, exacerbate menopausal symptoms, and lessen sexual desire.

HEALING OUR INNER CHILD

Mom, you were so busy with your career that you never had the time to tell me you loved me.
You listened to me only when I was sick or doing what made you proud.
You let me have only the feelings that pleased you. I only mattered to you when I did something that pleased you.
You never loved me for who I am.
I felt so lonely.

These were the words Sia said when I interviewed her and asked her to share how her mom made her feel. Her voice cracked, and she began to cry as she uttered these words. The wall of control she had carefully maintained for forty-three years began to fall with her tears. I embraced her and told her it was okay to cry. And then I praised her for her courage.

Although Sia had moved on, she was feeling the residual anger in her wounded inner child and just wanted to cry out in rage and anger. The sadness and loneliness she experienced in her childhood overwhelmed her. How could she ever recover from so much grief?

Yet, at the end of our interview, her bad mood changed to peace and joy, and she thanked me for helping her find and heal her wounded inner child.

I've learned over time that when an adult's development is hampered during their childhood, and their emotions (particularly hurt and anger) are suppressed, the child inside the adult remains angry and hurt. As a result, the adult's mature behavior will unintentionally become contaminated by their inner child.

Our inner child is that part of our subconscious mind that holds onto our memories and experiences, even when we might have forgotten them. Our inner child can dictate how we respond to certain events based on past experiences and memories.

Of course, sometimes we feel sad, scared, anxious, uncertain, depressed, or overwhelmed with indescribable emotions. Indeed, this loss of our innate potential is the biggest tragedy. And it's just as John Bradshaw said: "the more we know about how we lost our spontaneous wonder and creativity, the more we can find ways to get them back." We may even be able to prevent this from happening to our children in the future.

GETTING TO THE ROOT OF MENTAL HEALTH DIFFICULTIES

This book aims to help you gain more awareness of your current mental health and show you how to end the guesswork and blame game. So allow me to invite you on a journey to explore your mental health. Here, you will find specific questions you must ask yourself regarding your mental health if you want to check in with yourself as regularly and live the life you truly desire. These questions are divided into two parts, so don't be in a rush to answer them. Instead, take your time, note down your responses, and be completely honest. If the answer to one question leads to more questions, write them down. You don't have to answer these questions all at once, so let's get started!

This first part consists of statements that cover six areas of life and require you to state "true" or "false" as your answer:

- **Sense of self questions:** I think of myself as a decent person. And while I believe that others respect me, I can still feel good about myself even if I disagree with them.
- **Sense of belonging questions:** I am surrounded by people who support me. I have good feelings about the people I interact with and the relationships I have with them.
- **Sense of meaning or purpose questions:** I feel satisfied after completing tasks and projects. I evaluate my worldviews and my convictions.
- **Emotional resilience questions:** When difficulties arise, I manage them reasonably well. Even though I acknowledge that I can't always control events, I still try to help.
- **Enjoyment and hope questions:** I view my life optimistically. I like who I am as a person.
- **Contribution questions:** My actions have consequences. I influence those around me.

Of course, feel free to add more statements to these areas if you think the ones I shared are insufficient.

Now, let's move to the second part. These self-reflection questions can help you track where you are currently with your mental health and require you to write down your answers in your journal:

- Have I developed new sleeping patterns? Do I have regular waking and sleeping hours? How would I characterize the type of sleep I get?
- How has my appetite changed recently—has it grown or diminished?
- Do I find it difficult to concentrate at work or in school? Can I focus on the tasks I wish to complete? Do I still enjoy doing things that usually make me happy?
- Am I spending as much time with my friends now as before? Spending time with my family would be nice. Am I separating myself from the people that matter to me?
- Do I think I'm keeping a healthy balance between my time, profession, physical activity, and the people I care about? What about other things that are significant to me?
- On a scale of 1 to 10, how relaxed am I? Is this more or less than the usual or just the same?
- Do I feel happy, anxious, satisfied, or sad?
- How do I feel in terms of my energy level after the day's work is over? Has my level of fatigue changed significantly?
- Am I experiencing any strong feelings or mood changes? Any breakdowns, panic attacks, or suicidal thoughts?

After answering these questions, endeavor to track them over time and check for any differences.

Finally, I know many of us are happy, affirmed, and fulfilled. We are not hiding from our pasts or holding grudges against others. We are in positive and healthy relationships with men or women; we are mothers and partners; we love our families and care for our bodies and fellow women. We treat ourselves and other people with respect. But if we are being honest, too many black women are still not living the lives of their dreams, and perhaps we are in the same boat ourselves. We are burdened, buried, walled off, and often downright hard.

Therefore, it is time for us to make a bold move to seek professional help so that our generation and the next generation do not have to be limited anymore. There is no shame in getting professional help, especially in the case of severe depression. Sometimes, we need a little helping hand, at least in the beginning, to figure out what we're dealing with and how to overcome it.

I understand that time and money may be short, so talk to any authors who found free mental health care specifically for black women. We have the Sad Girls Club, Black Journalists' Therapy Relief Fund, Therapy for Black Girls, Loveland Foundation, and Boris Lawrence Henson Foundation, among others. So do not hesitate to check them out. You want to be better for the next generation of young black women. They need to know that you are more than the sum of our hurts. You don't want them to see you as damaged or broken. Instead, you want them to see that you are unique and worthy of love, respect, and adoration.

KEY POINTS

- We must carefully understand the state of our mental health and see how we can create awareness, reduce the stigma against black women with mental illnesses, and improve access to healthcare.
- Traumatic events we experience, whether during our childhood or as adults, can leave a lasting impact on our lives.
- Trauma symptoms linger or worsen in the days, weeks, or months following the traumatic event, resulting in PTSD.
- Race-based traumatic stress (RBTS) causes racial trauma. RBTS describes how you respond to mental and emotional hurt caused by gloomy race-related encounters—that is, systemic racism.
- Our menstrual cycle and the frequency of our periods can both be impacted by chronic stress. Additionally, they may interfere with conception, exacerbate menopausal symptoms, and lessen sexual desire.
- When an adult's development is hampered during their childhood, and their emotions (particularly hurt and anger) are suppressed, the child inside the adult remains angry and hurt. As a result, the adult's mature behavior will unintentionally become contaminated by their inner child.

3

RECOVERING FROM THE PAST AND CHANGING YOUR MINDSET

"You can fall, but you can rise also."

— ANGELIQUE KIDJO

Now that you know how poor mental health and the lack of self-care can steal your joy and happiness, it's time to start working on pulling yourself through without kicking and screaming. But over time, I have realized that the problem with most of us is that we want to eliminate the pain, fear, frustration, conflict, and negativity clouding our thinking while holding on to our old mindsets.

Of course, you want to feel self-fulfilled rather than rely on external signs of success for fulfillment. But how can you do that when you haven't changed your mindset and old belief system? No, it doesn't work that way—unless you want to continue going in circles.

To recover from your past and see the world differently, you must be willing to change your mindset. Yes, it starts there because recovering from your past and current ordeal requires a willingness to do specific tasks and attain certain goals. Therefore, you must let go of the past, broaden your mindset, and dissolve the fear in your mind. And to do this, you need to eliminate the arrogance that promotes crazy black super-woman mindsets like, "I can do everything alone. I don't need anyone."

Yes, doing everything yourself might make you strong, but at what cost?

Does it guarantee your happiness?

Of course, not!

Such belief only excuses the rest of the world from contributing to the happiness you deserve. So you must drop it and start working your way to recovery by building a self-care routine. That way, you'll heal faster, laugh more often, and treat yourself better.

While several pathways lead to putting the past behind you and changing your mindset, this chapter is aimed at helping you transform your stressful life into one filled with self-care and self-love. Essentially, it shares practical applications of the steps you should take to let go of your past and current challenges. It will also show you how to remove negative thinking blocks and overcome self-sabotaging behaviors like perfectionism and procrastination.

START BY LISTENING TO YOUR INNER CHILD

In Chapter 2, we talked about our inner child and how they are a part of our subconscious. As black women, we must look inward to see how we can connect with our inner child and champion them to become a valuable tool for self-love, healing, and experiencing joy and peace in our lives. Though it may be challenging at first, finding your inner child can help you develop positive traits you can use to move on with your life goals.

Connecting with and listening to your inner child involves reflecting on different stages of your life and asking deep questions. The best place to start is the day you were born. Then, you can travel down memory lane and visualize yourself as a mentor helping your younger self adapt to the world. As you do this, you'll evaluate your past choices and mistakes, which will help you make better decisions in the future.

Now, you may find it hard to imagine your inner child accurately, but you just have to look deep inside you. However, if you do this and still struggle to picture your inner child, then imagine them as part of your subconscious rather than your younger self. Yes, you can visualize your inner child as part of your subconscious because it has been gathering messages long before you were old enough to understand anything. Moreover, your subconscious mind contains hopes and dreams for the future, feelings, experiences, and beliefs from the past.

So let's look at some ways you can connect with and listen to your inner child:

- Practice mindfulness to become more self-aware
- Surround yourself with young people who will help you rediscover your younger self
- Reflect on the memories you cherished as a child
- Keep a journal to process your feelings

Finding your inner child can help you understand your experience as an adult. Unfortunately, tapping into the emotions you experienced as a youth can be hard. But you can always consult a therapist to help you connect with your inner child—a therapist who can teach you techniques for identifying stress and negative emotional triggers.

Now that you have discovered the simple steps to finding your inner child, the next stage is to ask your inner child specific questions like the ones below:

- How old was I when I experienced these emotions? What was the experience like for me?
- Do I remember the sensations I experienced then and how they made me feel?
- Did any triggers make me feel this way?
- What feelings did I arouse when I was a child?
- What's my inner child's worldview?
- In what ways has technology evolved since I was a child?
- What life lessons have I learned from my childhood?

- Did I have dreams as a child? If so, what were they?
- What have I always wished to be?
- What subjects did I enjoy studying the most?
- Whom did I grow up with as friends? Why did I decide to hang out with them?
- What did I find so fascinating as a child?
- Do I now perceive kids differently?
- When were my happiest moments, and with whom?
- Do I have any amusing tales from my youth?
- What are some funny and embarrassing experiences I don't want to forget?
- Can I embrace my inner child all the way?
- Does my inner child communicate with me?
- When was the last time I showed my inner child some love?
- How do I let go of the past?

Each of those questions demands particular kinds of nourishment. As you find answers to these questions, you can learn to give yourself that kind of nourishment. Later, as you learn how to champion your inner child, you will feed it with what it needs now to grow.

And if you are experiencing racial trauma caused by RBTS, as explained in Chapter 1, you should build a connection with your mind and body and practice radical self-care to help you heal.

Racial trauma may not inflict an injury directly on our body, but it is undoubtedly a psycho-physical experience. The body remembers! And the mind stores the memory.

Racially traumatic events traumatize the body and the mind, triggering several emotions. Also, each emotion is expressed differently, especially in how it manifests physically; thus, your emotions are cues to the areas you should focus on. Some of the signs of racial trauma include the following:

- Intrusive thoughts, flashbacks, difficulty concentrating, and irritability
- Low self-esteem, self-concept, and self-confidence
- Powerlessness, helplessness, fear, hopelessness, feelings of mistrust, and betrayal
- Shame, self-blame, guilt, and rejection
- Worthlessness and confused sense of self
- Body aches and fatigue
- Difficulty falling or staying asleep
- Increased substance abuse and binge-eating
- Outbursts of anger, sadness, and difficulty concentrating
- Generalized anxiety, panic attacks, and depression
- Suicidal thoughts and feelings

Now, here is a radical self-care recovery and wellness procedure you can use to heal from racial trauma:

- **Narrate your story safely and respectfully:** Undoubtedly, racial trauma devalues our personhood, especially for black women. So you must respect your sacred space, create a safe environment, tap into your inner resources such as strength, values, and spirituality and only talk to people you trust to help reestablish your sense of worthiness. You should also ask your family, friends, and support group for assistance. Also consult a therapist for professional help.

- **Respect your wants and experiences:** We all have unique needs and experiences, so define your short- and long-term self-care goals based on your needs, resources, capability, and capacity while considering your overall well-being, action plans, and available tools. Additionally, you should maintain a healthy distance from toxic people (especially racists) and places. Finally, you may use kind, encouraging words to heal from past hurt.

- **Identify and verbally communicate your emotions:** Racial trauma can leave you emotionally bewildered, but working with a therapist or counselor will teach you how to recognize and acknowledge these sensations. Additionally, psychotherapy can help you heal and restore your sense of trust and community.

- **Control your rage:** Anger is your body's way of warning you that something wrong has happened and that you must defend yourself. You will learn how to identify what triggers your anger and how you express anger. You'll also learn how to use your anger constructively by addressing and working through racial trauma.

- **Create a healthy lifestyle, mentality, and habits:** Try to develop healthy routines for your diet, sleep, sex, relationships, work, hobbies, and social life—one effective way to do this is to undergo cognitive behavioral therapy (CBT).

- **Relax your muscles:** Reducing stress and inner generational difficulties will help you live healthier by reducing various physical symptoms. Some effective relaxation methods include deep breathing, body scan meditation, mindfulness meditation, prayer, yoga and other related exercises, guided imagery, and visualization.

I have endured multiple racial traumas in various contexts as a woman of color. And over time, I've learned that racial trauma can be just as devastating as physical abuse. Racial trauma survivors have invisible emotional and cognitive wounds, physical suffering, and broken bones in their souls that need to be healed.

Overall, connecting with your inner child is a Zen-like experience. Children are natural Zen masters; their world is always brand-new. For the unwounded child, wonder is natural, and life is a mystery to unravel. Therefore, going back in time to connect with your inner child will fill your life with wonder again.

REWIRING YOUR BRAIN AFTER YEARS OF NEGATIVE SELF-TALK

I once tallied and evaluated the average number of positive and negative emotions we black women experience. In the end, one fact my findings pointed out is that negative emotions are usually stronger than positive ones. Scientists call this the negativity bias.

You see, your brain prefers predictability, certainty, and control. So when things are uncertain, and you have no idea what's going to happen next, your brain tries to make up an ending. Basically, it writes its narrative, which presents two problems. First, this narrative is often inaccurate. Secondly, it is usually negative, and negative thoughts damage our self-perception.

Thoughts like

"He'll never like a lady like me because I am black."
"People will think I'm stupid and boring."
"It's impossible to let go of the past."
"I'll never be successful."
"I'll never find someone who loves me."
"I'll die alone."

Do you see the constant theme in these statements? They are all negative predictions that can do some serious damage when left unchecked.

So simply put, the negativity bias is a cognitive prejudice that causes negative thoughts and feelings to have a more significant psychological impact than positive ones. Even when these negative and positive thoughts and feelings are of equal size, negativity bias still exists, making us more sensitive to negativity.

When negativity bias occurs, our brain is wired to notice and remember negative events and information over positive ones. For instance, you may notice that unhappy memories from your childhood are much stronger than happy ones. Or, if you're married, you may remember bad times—like all the fights you and your spouse have gotten into—over good times. And most of us can rattle off dozens of negative stories about work, but only a few positive stories.

Understanding the negativity bias is critical because it doesn't affect just what we remember from the past but also how we see the future. Consistently, research has shown that negative self-talk is linked to tension and anxiety and that negative self-talk after failure or setback frequently results in lower self-confidence.

Most importantly, research indicates that negative self-talk lowers one's ability to accomplish goals. Because of the negativity bias, we tend to talk more negatively and predict doom, gloom, mayhem, and failure. And this leads to fear, making us feel stuck. There's no denying that the influence of negativity bias on our decision-making, internal motivation, and interpersonal interactions is profound.

So how do you avoid negativity bias?

The first step is to recognize how negativity bias might creep into your thoughts and decision-making process, and that's what we've just covered. As you become more aware of your thoughts and feelings, you can practice the following four habits to overcome negative self-talk and prevent negativity bias:

The Noticing, Naming, and Non-Identifying Habit

When you always speak and think negatively, the first and most crucial step to overcoming this problem is to become aware of it and mentally separate yourself from that mindset. The process is as follows:

- Firstly, the "voice" of your negative self-talk needs a name, so you can give it a funky name, like "Miss Negativity," to put mental and emotional distance between you and it
- Next, recognize the moments you mostly talk or think about yourself negatively
- Finally, consciously stop the negative self-talk and avoid identifying with it. For instance, you may say, "Here is Miss Negativity again," or "This isn't me talking." Statements like these can cause you to pause and reform your negative habits and mindset.

Although this process sounds simple, you may find it challenging to do. So prepare for progress and regressions and plan consistent repetitions.

The Self-Reassuring Habit

Positive self-talk is crucial to the self-reassuring habit. Telling yourself, "I've got this. It's not the end of the world," is a great way to reassure yourself. Here are some other things you can use to reinforce the self-reassuring habit:

- Talk to yourself as you would a trusted friend, well-wisher, or coworker; this triggers the parts of your brain that controls empathy.
- Consider the circumstance or setback, examine it, draw lessons from it, and then de-catastrophize it
- Speak kindly to yourself constantly and take an active role in being your champion and supporter

The Self-Compassion Habit

Self-compassion is our rocket fuel for enhancing motivation, growth mindset, peak performance, and well-being. It simply entails being kind to yourself during hard times and accepting that making mistakes is a necessary part of the learning process. If you want to be kinder to yourself, you should do the following:

- Always maintain a positive attitude and self-image
- Try to find solace in the idea that others have also gone through a similar situation, so you are not alone
- Be aware of the bad experience and consciously let it go

Self-compassion inspires us to improve, bounce back from past failures, and perform better. It also improves our well-being and happiness while reducing stress and anxiety. However, keep in mind that the concept of self-compassion can initially feel foreign and even frightening when we have a strong negative self-talk tendency. That's quite normal, but it's not enough reason to give up.

The "Stay-at-it" Habit

The practice of "staying at it" has its roots in early life. Neuroscientists have demonstrated that "neurons that fire together, wire together," and we can alter our thought patterns by affirming positive thoughts repeatedly. So keep going—keep these practices in mind every day. There needs to be a lot of rewiring, but the benefits outweigh the costs.

So whenever negative thoughts arise, shift your focus to kind, hopeful, or even funny thoughts. Also, curb your habit of fueling negativity with more negativity. Instead of wallowing in all that negativity, counter it with a positive mindset. That way, you'll be well on your way to overcoming negative self-talk.

SELF-SABOTAGING BEHAVIOR

At this point, you might be thinking misfortune always finds you. It's anyone else's fault but yours. But if this is a lifelong pattern, chances are there is a self-sabotager sharing your body with you.

One of the hardest facts in life is that nobody gets in our way as often as we do. There are significant roadblocks we put in place and stand solidly behind while positive traffic gets detoured in the other direction.

There are the more obvious ones: food, gambling, sex, booze, and drugs. Those are the ones that have more evident physical and psychological manifestations. We get called out on them.

People might whisper behind our backs, instigate interventions, or hurl ultimatums, like "Stop right there, or else . . ."

But there are also more subtle ones that we might casually refer to as our quirks: "You know me; there I go again." But the logical next phase of questions and answers seldom occurs: "Why did I go there again? And what choice took me there?"

Excavation is not so often on our to-do list regarding these deep-rooted, life-limiting behaviors. These quirks, issues, misdemeanor, negative character traits, and self-sabotaging ways often get us saying things like:

"Oh, my life tilts toward a long line of poor choices that constantly leave me exactly where I don't want to be."
"Damn! It's like the heavens are shining on everyone else and spitting on me."
"I shouldn't bother trying to please Janet; she will find fault in whatever I do."

Sound familiar?

Ask yourself a simple question and answer it honestly: Am I unconsciously creating failure?

What is it about you? Do you have a self-limiting mindset? And where do you go again and again? Are you happy there? If not, then why do you keep returning there?

What makes you feel at home and comfy even though it causes you pain and gets you no closer to where you want to be? Oh, and one more thing: where do you want to be?

Outside of random bad luck, much of our lives are the sum of our choices. If we choose to find fault, trip ourselves up, and not leverage our advantages, we need to look in a mirror and yell, "Something needs to change, and it's probably me."

This brief self-sabotage quiz below could help you pinpoint the self-limiting mindsets and behavioral habits that are holding you back. So read through the patterns outlined and rate how applicable each is to you on a scale of 1–10. A rating of 1 means "Not a problem at all," and 7 means "This is a big problem for me." You surely need to work on getting a rating of 5 and above.

Ready? Let's dive in:

- You don't set aside time or mental space to transform your life, yet you expect yourself to succeed.
- You believe that other people's actions determine your ability to change.
- You're a perfectionist who ignores gradual progress and is only content until a problem is entirely resolved.
- You establish self-imposed regulations that encourage procrastination.
- You overcomplicate solutions to problems. To come up with the ideal solution, you contemplate and research nonstop.
- You're too busy to devise methods or processes to manage your time more effectively.
- You skip out on simple joys and downtime to watch Netflix until 3 a.m.
- You disregard the cues that you need a break.

- You refrain from acting on your desires because you believe that you can't achieve them. For instance, you may think you must lose weight before enrolling in a dance class.
- Instead of taking the effort to set up a password manager, you waste a lot of time and mental energy reinventing the wheel, such as repeatedly changing forgotten passwords.
- People in your life defer to you for all decisions rather than sharing some responsibility. Instead of allowing them to use their judgment, you support this tendency.
- In situations where you have the option to be happy or unhappy, you decide to be unhappy.
- You continue acting in psychologically comfortable ways despite being unhelpful to you.
- You don't hold yourself accountable for using the proper problem-solving techniques when you allow yourself to ruminate or worry.
- When a relationship has to be improved, you tend to place too much emphasis on reducing unpleasant interactions while placing too little emphasis on fostering positive interactions and shared experiences.
- From your glass mansion, you fling stones and complain about other people's behaviors when yours need improving.
- You repeatedly use ineffective persuasion techniques that fail 90% of the time.
- When other people raise legitimate concerns about your behavior, you choose to ignore them. For instance, even though your partner has a point when they

criticize you for spending time on unimportant things, you fail to accept this.

- You make decisions instead of dealing with reality based on how you imagine a situation should be.
- When your past traumas and hurts resurface, you lack practical tools to help you control your emotions and behavior.
- You cause tension for yourself. For example, you begin more projects than you have time to complete.
- You complete low-priority chores while putting off high-important ones.
- You overwork when you genuinely need to take a step back and view the larger picture.
- When self-acceptance and compassion might positively affect your behavior and feelings, you choose to be self-critical instead.
- When your financial decisions don't make sense, you base them on being persuaded by marketing incentives. For example, because you earn loyalty points from one hotel chain, you'll pay $60 extra to stay there even though the points are only worth $20 to $35.
- You continue to pay for memberships that you hardly ever use.

Now, study your answers' ratings and work on those you've rated 5 or above. Once you know your patterns, you'll see obvious avenues for change in most situations. Here are tips you can use to overcome those self-sabotaging patterns:

- If taking the quiz gave you a lot of "that's me" moments, choose the thing you want to work on the most or concentrate on the habits that have the most damaging effects on your life and relationships
- Make clear behavioral goals for what you'll start doing after identifying your tendencies. For instance, you may employ two tactics if pessimism negatively impacts your relationships. First, you may resolve to speak positively at least once at each meeting you attend at work, and you make it a point to compliment your spouse the moment you see them each evening.
- Any behavior modification strategy you develop requires a contextual trigger. For example, "When I see my spouse, I'll mention something pleasant about her" means, "When X happens, I'll do Y."

Instead of eradicating all self-defeating behavior from your life, you should seek to enhance your behaviors by, say, 5, 10, or 20%. Believe it or not, small changes over time will help you rewire your default attitudes to develop tenacious new habits. This brings us to the next part.

DEALING WITH PROCRASTINATION AND PERFECTIONISM

Culture is often to blame for procrastination, as we black women feel the societal pressure to take care of others before ourselves, causing us to overlook certain activities. You know, we often hear people say that if you think and care about yourself, you're selfish. However, that is untrue.

And if you try to stop procrastinating, you might be startled to find out that it involves more than just putting things aside. For instance, we tell ourselves we'll slaughter this beast at the start of the year. So we write lists, buy notebooks, and experiment with new things. Still, no matter what we do, we frequently follow the same pattern of delaying and avoiding, repeatedly rescheduling hobbies, like vacations, and necessities, like doctor's appointments. And most times, it is because we don't have quick rewards, as we tend to prioritize short-term results over long-term goals.

So what do you do to overcome procrastination?

First, work on splitting everyday tasks into smaller, more attainable objectives. Then, for a short predetermined time, let's say 20 minutes, work on them.

Make a list of the tasks you want to complete the following day at the end of each workday. List them in ascending order of significance. The next day, focus on those issues and none other.

The best way to accomplish a task is to use your natural patterns to your advantage; that is, find out where your energy levels are higher during certain times of the day and prioritize your tasks accordingly. For instance, you should do the most challenging tasks in the morning if that's when your energy level is at its highest.

Finally, celebrating even your smallest successes is a massive motivator to overcome procrastination. So be kind to yourself. According to research, self-compassion might help you manage the stress caused by procrastination. Always remember that every success, big or small, is just what it is—a success!

Meanwhile, several studies have also connected procrastination and perfectionism. And this is true, especially for black women, as they often feel the need to do everything perfectly and according to society's standards. Over time, this can be so overwhelming that it stops us from accomplishing our set goals.

So while you try to deal with procrastination, you also want to ensure that you work on overcoming perfectionism. Here are 3 ways to do so:

- **There is nothing wrong with asking for help when you need it:** Asking an expert for help or advice regarding a new task can help you advance your efforts and make significant progress. That said, if you are experiencing mental and emotional difficulty due to events in your life, you could seek counseling to help you work through it. You mustn't do everything on your own.
- **Please don't wait until you have a clear picture:** It's totally okay to start from the bottom. In fact, Oprah Winfrey wouldn't be where she is today if she hadn't started from the bottom. As perfectionists, we tend to assume that we will learn new habits and skills flawlessly on the first try, which is hardly ever the case for anyone. So take a step back and try again if you are learning something new and have trouble perfecting your form. If you make mistakes, allow yourself to learn

from them. After all, you can't get better if you don't have room to grow.

- **Love yourself and your situation, as-is**: At one point or another, you probably must have said things like, "Until I do or can accomplish so-and-so, I'll never be happy." I understand because I used to struggle with this too, and honestly, it sucks. This mindset is so destructive because after you achieve anything you set out to do, you will instantly turn your attention to another goal. As a result, it creates a vicious cycle that can lead directly to anxiety and despair. So kill this mindset and work on loving yourself and your life the way it is now.

OVERCOMING GUILT AND LEARNING TO FORGIVE

Guilt and shame are common feelings we as black women experience when we examine white privileges and remember how they have oppressed us for centuries, especially in terms of prejudice and racial discrimination.

Guilt is the discomfort you feel after doing something wrong. Meanwhile, shame is what you feel when you fail to live up to your ideals. While guilt tells you that you have done something wrong and need to do something about it, shame can make you feel exposed as a bad person and see yourself as incapable of change.

When guilt and shame keep us from having genuine relationships, we maintain our stereotypes, fears, and ignorance. But we need to know each other as unique human beings and not just as members of an ethnic group.

To overcome these emotions, there needs to be some self-exploration, self-awareness, and internal dialogue, much of which we have already begun to explore. Confronting your guilt and shame can help you feel positive about yourself. Instead of reacting blindly to uncomfortable feelings, you increase your ability to think independently and stand up against oppression in its many forms. You can then take full responsibility for your actions, own up to your mistakes, learn from them, forgive and let go.

Forgiveness, like grace, is the willingness to see a situation or person from a much higher perspective. It invites bold change. The deliberate process of forgiveness is to cease the feelings of resentment against an offender and can be very strenuous and complicated. When we forgive ourselves, we give up our desire to punish ourselves by allowing room for our mistakes, flaws, and weaknesses.

Here are suggested steps you can take to overcome guilt and forgive yourself:

- Accept responsibility for your actions if you've been justifying them
- Describe what happened in detail, including your thoughts and those of the other participants before, during, and after the event
- Examine the principles, values, and criteria you use to evaluate yourself. Are they yours or that of your family,

friends, spouse, or followers of your faith? Do you require their consent?

- Did your behavior align with your core principles? If not, identify the thoughts, feelings, and beliefs that motivated it.
- How did your deeds impact you and other people? Whom did you hurt? Put your name on the list.
- Consider ways to apologize, then take action
- Write a kind letter of acceptance, gratitude, and repentance to yourself
- Finally, describe what you did to others. Don't divulge to anyone who might criticize you. You can consult a therapist, your family, or close friends.

Recognize that you can forgive yourself even if you still feel you did something wrong, just as you can forgive someone else even if you believe they did something wrong. You can acknowledge your mistakes and express regret for what you did. Given your circumstances, awareness, maturity, and experience at the time, you may have done your best. This is a good, modest attitude.

SELF-CARE ASSESSMENT EXERCISE II

In this assessment exercise, here is what you need to do:

- First, write down at least 5 negative thoughts or experiences; they don't necessarily have to be about racism.

- With the steps you have learned in this chapter, analyze these negative feelings to see if they are valid and work on replacing them with positive ones

Of course, you must regularly practice this exercise until the positive thoughts become more natural.

Now, I understand that replacing our negative thoughts with positive ones isn't as easy as it sounds. So to help out with that, we will look at rediscovering who we are at this stage of the journey in the next chapter. We will also work together to discover the power of writing and positive affirmations and how they can lead us toward a happier life.

So I invite you to join me on a journey to putting the past behind you. A journey of forgiveness, healing, good health, emotional balance and wellness, financial security, self-love, sisterly love, romantic love, and reconnection with your true self will allow you to embrace all of you in all of your splendor and majesty.

KEY POINTS

- Connecting with and listening to your inner child involves reflecting on different stages of your life and asking deep questions.
- Understanding the negativity bias is critical because it doesn't affect just what we remember from the past but also how we see the future.

- Procrastination is linked with perfectionism. And this is true, especially for black women, as they often feel the need to do everything perfectly and according to society's standards.
- Confronting your guilt and shame can help you feel positive about yourself.

4

REDISCOVERING WHO YOU ARE AND DEFINING YOUR HAPPINESS

"Your willingness to look at your darkness is what empowers you to change."

— IYANLA VANZANT

M ost of the strong black women I come across go through life believing that their happiness or unhappiness is primarily determined by the events in their environment and people's expectations of them. I get it.When you have the pressure of being a strong black woman on your shoulders, it's easy to feel that your purpose in life is to please society. You want to earn an income to raise a family. You want to continue the fight of those before you to achieve gender equality. And you want to fulfill these purposes no matter the level of self-sacrifice you have to take.

Yes, financial independence and raising a family are indeed important dreams to realize, but they don't define you. After all, before you were so-and-so's partner or so-and-so's mom, you were you!

In one of my interviews with Barbara, she talked about how hard it was for her to experience happiness, become self-fulfilled, and lead a balanced life. And then, one Thursday night, as she and her step-mom did the dishes, they had deep conversations. "It's a common routine for the both of us, and we enjoy it," Barbara explained.

At 33, Barbara had many ups and downs and sometimes felt strange. She said she sometimes felt like an elastic band that was being stretched beyond its elastic limit. However, Barbara was very reflective at the time, just trying to figure out how she could let go of her suppressing emotional baggage and feel lighter.

During one of these deep conversations, Barbara expressed her feelings to her mom. And her mom replied, "Barbara, have you ever stopped to think about what happiness truly means to you? Perhaps, you need to take some time to rediscover yourself and then look deep within and around you to see all the things you have to be thankful for. There will always be people whose lives seem to be better or worse than yours, but stop and think of the things you can be grateful for."

After some reflection, Barbara replied to her mom, "You know, there really are more things to be grateful for than to be sad about." Barbara's brief conversation with her mom that night encouraged her to focus and reflect more on her happiness.

Although she knew she had to put in the effort, she saw that there was so much more to life and her future.

I believe that gratitude inspires pure joy, and I doubt there has ever been a day in any strong black woman's life that there was nothing to be grateful for. In varying degrees, you must realize that rediscovering who you are and defining your happiness is like rain to a field of wildflowers; you only blossom when you release yourself from the negative thoughts and feelings holding you back.

But why do this kind of work within yourself? Even though it may be very clear, it needs to be stated: we may struggle with some of the things we do—with whatever personally compromises us or our satisfaction in life—so that we might achieve greater freedom. Seen in this light, you can boldly say that letting go of the past and negativity and looking closer at what it means for you to be happy is an act of self-care.

LOVE YOUR TRUE SELF

There is a difference between wanting personal growth and making improvements to accept yourself as who you are and will always strive to be. Loving yourself is the first and only path to infusing love into your life and everything you do.

Self-love is the personal commitment of strong black women to slowing down enough to embrace stillness, healing, and renewal as a daily part of their lives. It also means nurturing and enriching every aspect of their lives: mind, body, and spirit.

Here are ten ways you can start practicing self-love:

- **Stay in the present:** Rather than spend time with your smartphone, trying to process the endless amounts of information it throws at you, pick one activity you love and be present while doing it. It could be crafting, coloring, journaling, or sharing a meal with your partner or friend.
- **Be open to learning:** Nothing is more stimulating than learning something new. Continuous and committed learning is an amazing way to build confidence. So you could take a class in a subject you want to learn more about or learn a new skill such as photography or writing.
- **Don't be afraid to say no:** I know we black women are so used to putting everyone else ahead of ourselves, which can be overwhelming. But did you know that every time you say yes to someone else's priorities over yours, you say no to yourself? Yes, that's right. So instead of immediately agreeing to every request, ask for time to thoroughly think about your response so you can ensure you aren't being selfish to yourself. There is nothing wrong with giving "no" as an answer.
- **Exercise daily:** This doesn't necessarily mean you have to do intense daily workouts. No! It can be as simple as periodically getting up and moving around your space daily. Resting a few minutes is another unique way to practice self-love and gratitude.
- **Eat nutritional meals:** Don't deprive yourself of nutritious meals or rely on junk that could accumulate

stress in your body. Your body thrives best when you eat a healthy mix of complex carbohydrates, protein, and fats. You also get enough energy to fuel your busy life.

- **Surround yourself with positivity:** We have already done justice by learning the steps required to get rid of negativity. But in addition to what you've learned, you should try to surround yourself with as many positive words as possible. For example, you can listen to inspiring songs full of positive, inspiring lyrics. You can also recite some positive affirmations (check the last section of this chapter for more details).

- **Dress well to feel confident:** Take some time to put a little extra thought into your outfit. Always wear your favorite hairstyle, and make sure your brows are perfectly curved. Do those little things that make you feel like the fantastic and strong black woman you are.

- **Share your talent and gifts:** You have unique gifts and talents that the world is dying to see. So do not hide your visions; reveal and share them! Even if they're just ideas, share them in a safe space with someone you trust. Believing in and sharing your gifts, ideas, and talents is an incredible act of self-love that can positively impact those around you.

- **Know your worth:** When was the last time you evaluated your self-worth? You must audit yourself every once in a while to ensure your life is constantly aligned with your values. Knowing your worth is also incredibly rewarding and a bold act of self-love.

- **Embrace your uniqueness:** If you think you aren't weird, you are lying to yourself. We all certainly have that weird little side, which makes us unique, so don't be afraid to love your quirky weirdness.

To help you on this journey, we will discuss some of these points in greater detail in subsequent chapters. Self-love is about taking away all the pressure and expectations you think people have about you and appreciating that you are unique and should be celebrated. A deeper sense of self-love leads the strong black woman to greater peace and happiness.

HOW TO DISCOVER YOUR PURPOSE

The purpose or meaning of life is a challenging question; without it, we can feel like we are behind the wheel of an automatic car with no specific direction. But with a clear purpose, leading a longer and happier life becomes easier.

Purpose is one of the fundamental keys we as strong black women need to fully grasp and pursue with all our time on earth if we desire to live fulfilled lives. Without purpose, defining our happiness will be a problem. It's not enough to have gifts or talents and the right mindset; how are you using your gifts? How are you applying your thought process? Are they helping you, your family, community, country, or the world?

Having great potential and incredible abilities will not do us any good until we use them to improve our lives and the lives of others. So how do you find your purpose? Well, here are five questions to ask yourself to help you discover your purpose:

1. What are the things I love?

What gives you even a small amount of joy? You probably have many things that make you happy, so try to list them. Anything that makes you happy, which you enjoy writing about, is worth the effort. I can promise you that there aren't any ridiculous or foolish responses.

All the incredible and sophisticated things you see around you now, like cars and airplane engines, were once simple concepts. Your life also began as an ordinary notion. I might not be able to tell you your purpose, but I can guarantee that it will reveal itself to you in the form of the things you adore that align with your passion. So asking yourself this fundamental question should be your first step.

2. What am I passionate about?

If you pay close attention to your list of things you enjoy, you may feel compelled to share some of them with your loved ones. You may pay attention to your eating habits and exercise routines, or you could pursue arts and crafts. You'll notice that you appear to talk about it nonstop. It consumes all your thoughts, even when nobody is paying attention and others around you are pleading to switch topics. Yes! That right there is your true purpose, so note it down.

3. What are my strengths and core skills?

We all have talents, capacities, and abilities we inherited at birth or learned through experience and training. So what are yours? What would you say if someone asked you to introduce yourself to your potential life partner or employer? Your life should be focused on a combination of your passions, values, skills, and talents.

4. Who is my role model?

Finding your life's purpose can sometimes be aided by looking to those you have admired at some point in the past. So consider all the people who have influenced you throughout your life. Whether it was a relative, professor, celebrity, activist, or fictional character, take note of their names.

Now look over the list. What particular traits do you find appealing about these people? What aspects of their behavior do you want to emulate? What virtues do you and them share? What aspects of their lives inspire you? What have they accomplished? Your answers could be the key to discovering your purpose.

5. How do I want to be remembered?

Everyone dies at some point, but how do you want to be remembered when you die? What are the things you know you'll reflect on and regret not doing when your life is almost over? Conversely, what are the things you know you'd be happy to have accomplished as you draw your last breath?

Death-related thoughts don't have to be morbid. They can be motivating if we use them to remind ourselves of life's transient nature and why we should live our lives to the fullest before it's too late.

Discovering your life's meaning requires creating rather than finding it. Your purpose, which is also your future, is always bigger than your present. You can't handle your future with your present ability, attitude, skills, and knowledge. So take action toward figuring out what makes life meaningful for you.

WHAT DOES YOUR ULTIMATE HAPPINESS LOOK LIKE?

It's sad that today, we can even feel guilty for being happy. For many of us, living as we do in a culture that embraces the "pleasure principle" over the principles of happiness has made us lose sight of the differences between happiness and pleasure. You may ask why many strong black women never seem to understand what ultimate happiness looks like. Perhaps, it's because of the suppression we face in society.

For many black women, being strong means being there through thick or thin, even if they don't get the same treatment from their loved and trusted ones. Unfortunately, because many of us have been conditioned to put up with a lot of silliness and drama in our world, we often don't allow ourselves to enjoy the ultimate happiness we deserve, desire, and are entitled to.

One way to learn what makes you happy is to collect information on a daily basis about how happy you are so that you can notice different patterns of things that make you happy. Here is how to go about it:

- **Rate your happiness each day:** Rate how happy you are on a scale of 1 to 10, where 1 means "depressed" and 10 means "excited." Try not to overthink it. Just recall how joyful you felt and record everything you did each day. If you can, determine what aspects of the day contributed to your happiness. Even if you're unsure of how some events may affect your happiness at the moment, try to document them in writing. Examples include "Worked on my diet" and "Spent time with my kids."
- **Analyze the numbers:** After creating the data, spend some time reviewing it. Start by reviewing your happiest days, then ask yourself what you did on those days. Next, do the same for your saddest days. Lastly, look for trends on happy and sad days to determine what makes you happy.
- **Take a happiness quiz:** Happiness quizzes are another way to measure your happiness. As simple as they may seem, they can guide you on the right path, though they usually offer more generic solutions than specific ones to help you determine what makes you happy. You can take several of these quizzes online.

- **Meditate for happiness:** Happiness can come from meditation since it makes you spend time alone with your thoughts and emotions. As you meditate, you might learn more about yourself, such as what makes you unhappy and what brings you the most joy.
- **Consult a therapist:** Once more, talking to a therapist can assist in determining what makes you happy. Therapists are qualified to assist in identifying your sources of happiness and resolve any problems causing you distress.

You don't have to wait for life to hit you hard before waking up to the possibility of absolute joy in your life. Instead, you can work each day toward creating and sustaining more inner peace and happiness in your life.

THE SCIENTIFIC REASON TO USE POSITIVE AFFIRMATIONS

Another tremendous tool to help strong black women live their dream lives is positive affirmations. Positive affirmations are short, inspiring sentences in the present tense that we repeat to ourselves to reform our mindsets. Beyoncé is known for her positive quotes and affirmations, like one where she says, "I dream it, I work hard, I grind 'til I own it."

And trust me, there is neuroscience research that backs its effectiveness. For example, a study published in *Social Cognitive and Affective Neuroscience* revealed what happens in our brains when we recite positive affirmations regularly. Using MRI, the researchers discovered that self-affirmation practice activates the brain's reward regions, the ventral striatum (VS), and the ventromedial prefrontal cortex (VMPFC). These regions are the same reward centers that react to other joyful experiences, like eating your favorite meal or winning a prize in a contest.

So you see, practicing self-affirmation does help in activating those areas of the brain that makes you joyful and feel positive feelings. Drafting statements of how we want to be, who we want to be, and the attributes we wish to possess, and then speaking these statements to ourselves and believing in their truth, leads to a place where anything is possible. Speaking healing, forgiveness, accomplishment, and success into your life can have a magical effect.

Here is a list of some of the most powerful affirmations for every black woman:

- *When I wake up, I am grateful to be a black woman.*
- *I am so proud to be a black woman. There is nothing else I would rather be.*
- *I say yes to myself even if others say no to me.*
- *If someone is staring too intently at me, they are trying to comprehend the wonder of who I am.*
- *I have massive affection for myself, and I will never doubt that.*
- *It's time to demonstrate to the world how magnificent I am—I was born with greatness.*
- *Being a black woman, I deserve to rest.*
- *I take such excellent care of myself that I am the ideal mother for my kids.*

- *I will not ignore warnings of burnout. My family needs me, and I need them.*
- *I firmly believe that my voice counts and that I merit attention. So please pay attention to what I say because it is always valid.*
- *I adore myself. I cherish every black woman. And I love how we invent simply by existing.*
- *I'm pleased that I've grown and said goodbye to things that no longer benefit me.*
- *Because my needs will always be essential, I owe it to myself to take care of myself.*
- *I will not crumble under pressure. Rather, practicing self-care will strengthen me.*
- *My fellow queens and those that love and support me are all around me.*
- *Being cheerful and black is the rule, not the exception.*
- *I will not give in to condescending words. People will listen when I voice my opinion.*
- *My goals are clear, and I have a promising future.*
- *I am a strong, capable person who radiates success. I deserve every ounce of joy, love, and happiness that I experience.*

Of course, you can create more positive affirmations yourself by following the basic rules. Simply take some time to review your passions, vision, mission, challenges you have faced, how you resolved them, and your dream life. Then ask yourself what affirmations you can design to actualize and manifest your ultimate life. Please remember to use convicting statements like "I will," "I have," and "I am," rather than "I want," "I hope," "I wish," etc. Your affirmations will change as you move forward each week and month. Create your statements so that they are aligned with your monthly calendar. Review them each week, and edit or add them as needed.

As you must have learned, while going over your past is a necessary part of self-care, it can leave you feeling as if you don't know who you are. Therefore, you must rediscover your purpose and what you want in life and seek out what makes you genuinely happy, not just what is expected of you.

Of course, this will positively impact your self-esteem. Still, you may experience some difficulties on this journey from those around you. It may be your loved ones or the annoying shop assistant who looks at your shampoo in a judgmental way. So what do you do? You need to find your assertive voice and learn how to harness its power. And that's our goal for the next chapter.

KEY POINTS

- Loving yourself is the first and only path to infusing love into your life and everything you do.
- Purpose is one of the fundamental keys we strong black women need to fully grasp and pursue with all our time on earth if we desire to live fulfilled lives.
- You don't have to wait for life to hit you hard before waking up to the possibility of absolute joy in your life. Instead, you can work each day toward creating and sustaining more inner peace and happiness in your life.

- Practicing self-affirmation does help in activating those areas of the brain that makes you happy and positive.

5

FINDING YOUR ASSERTIVE VOICE

"In order to have enough of me to share, I cannot keep giving all my pieces."

— UNKNOWN

To whom or what do you dedicate most of your time, energy, and attention to? Is it your career, friends, partner, kids, or household chores? I've noticed that we black women tend to give too much of ourselves because we are afraid to be assertive, which could easily lead to burnout.

A recent study revealed that black American women age faster when they repeatedly or consistently adjust to subjective and objective pressures. Using information from the Study of Women's Health Across the Nation (SWAN), it was estimated that at ages 49–55, black women are 7.5 years biologically "older" than white women. When you look at this data, you can easily see why you need to find your voice, take a stand, and be more assertive in your life.

My friend, Jackie, once told me about how she enrolled in a black-and-white photography class at a local arts center in downtown Fort Lauderdale. Once a week, she rushed from her office and fought congested traffic to make it to her class in time.

However, one evening, she got to class late. So she apologized to her instructor, who was about twice her age, for being late and tried to explain her travails to him. To Jackie's surprise, her instructor shrugged and said, "Well, that was your choice." Frustrated, Jackie explained her ordeal further so he could better understand her predicament.

"No, you don't get it!" she said. "Today, I led a media tour for the press, attended four meetings, answered several phone calls, and replied to many emails." Still, her instructor smiled at her and said, "It was your choice, Jackie."

Jackie got upset and still wanted to prove her point, as she thought her instructor had lost touch with reality. But then she realized he was right. As annoying as the instructor's words were, they sunk in, and she realized she had a choice after all.

And the same applies to all of us black women. We all have a choice. For instance, you may have tried to recover from the past and set your priorities right. But now is the time to put your life in order, define boundaries, and learn to say no to bad choices that will only deter you.

This chapter aims to help you improve your daily life and relationships to assert your discoveries. Here, you will learn how to say no, create and communicate boundaries, and check in on your body language and communication skills, which are crucial to your personal and professional development. But before we proceed, let's take a closer look at emotional self-care.

GETTING GOOD AT EMOTIONAL SELF-CARE

Our feelings and how we express them can either boost or weaken our immune system. The connection between emotions and illnesses stems from how we process and cope with emotions and, sometimes, how we avoid them.

So expressing your feelings instead of stifling them is an example of healthy emotional self-care; making out time to have fun is another. On the other hand, being stuck in a routine can make you feel bored or low. However, when you switch things up now and again, you will positively impact your emotional life and boost your self-esteem. Below are some emotional self-care activities for black women to try:

- **Pay attention to your body:** You can take care of your emotions by paying attention to your body. So take note of how your emotions affect you physically. For example, do they make you feel drained or energized?
- **Ask for help before you need it:** It's never a bad idea to ask for help when you need it. However, asking for help *before* you need it gives the people you're asking enough

time to prepare and adequately help you, whether what you need is moral support or someone you can vent to.

- **Practice mindfulness:** Take a moment to sit and breathe while experiencing your emotions. Your feelings are what they are; they are not good or terrible, right or wrong. Simply allowing your feelings to exist is a crucial component of emotional self-care.

- **Consciously choose how to respond:** While we have no control over what happens to us, we have a say in how we react to it. You have the power to take a deep breath, treat yourself and others with kindness, and discover methods to remain calm and optimistic; whether you're dealing with a pandemic, sickness, or whiny toddler.

- **Stay connected to others:** Take regular breaks from the news and your phone to engage in pleasant, healthy activities with others around you. We black women need strong connections and support systems to protect our sanity. So spend time with people who make you laugh or binge-watch that latest comedy TV series. In the end, laughter will boost our immune system, lower stress levels, and elevate our mood.

- **Practice gratitude:** We can exercise emotional self-care by focusing on what is right instead of wrong. You may elevate your mood and reduce stress by incorporating gratitude into your everyday routine.

- **Engage in a relaxing hobby:** What hobbies interest you the most? Do you enjoy photography or painting? What about that once-loved hobby you've now given up? Concentrating on an enjoyable, peaceful hobby is an excellent way to unwind and clear your mind. Now is a perfect opportunity to do anything you've always wanted to do!

Your emotional health deserves just as much attention as your physical health, which we will cover in the next chapter. So consider including at least one emotional self-care exercise into your daily routine and see the difference. You should treat yourself with the utmost respect.

THE BALANCE BETWEEN PASSIVE, AGGRESSIVE, AND ASSERTIVE COMMUNICATION

Being assertive—acting in a decisive and self-confident manner —is an essential aspect of healthy emotional self-care. However, there are significant differences between being passive, aggressive, and assertive.

For instance, passiveness is being lethargic, scared to stand up for yourself, and overly submissive at your expense, especially regarding important matters that affect you. One way to know you're passive is that you settle for less when you could treat yourself better.

Passive people don't express their displeasure or hurt at things directly. Instead, they allow resentment to build up and are usually oblivious to the accumulation. But once they exhaust their patience and tolerance for what's causing them displeasure, they are prone to explosive outbursts, which are often excessive compared to the incident that set them off. However, after the outburst, they could experience remorse, embarrassment, and confusion, which makes them revert to being passive again.

Usually, when black women are passive, people see them as weak and worthless. Over time, this could make them resent themselves and those around them.

Aggression is acting too intensely and being violent when interacting with others. Thus, aggressive communicators have verbally and physically abusive body language. For example, they may be constantly defensive, resistant to whatever is said or done, or overly reactive. When you are too aggressive toward others, people will avoid you.

Neither passiveness nor aggression are healthy approaches to relationships and will only isolate you from people. But when you're assertive, you choose to take a stand and calmly express yourself without attacking the other person. Shonda Rhimes displayed assertiveness perfectly when she spoke her mind about the New York Times article that described her as an "angry black woman." As the creator of shows like *Grey's Anatomy* and *Scandal*, she has changed how we view black women on television.

Alessandra Stanley, a New York Times critic, attempted to compliment Rhimes for how she has "reset the image of African-American women on television." But instead, Stanley caused an uproar with the opening paragraph of her article: "When Rhimes writes her autobiography, it should be titled *How to Get Away With Being an Angry Black Woman.*"

So Rhimes publicly complained about why she would be labeled an "angry black woman" when her angry white characters weren't. "It's not enough that we have to put up with the strong black woman, but we also have to deal with the "angry black woman stereotype"," Rhimes stated. "Why does everyone need to bring up race and gender when discussing me?"

Expressing your feelings in a way that does not attack the character of others is highly beneficial when building your confidence and that of others. Here are a few tips on how to become more assertive:

- Confidently express your mind
- Be open-minded, consider other people's suggestions, make a decision, and take action
- Thank people when they give you a compliment
- Participate in an activity, even though you may feel a little uncomfortable

As a black woman, when you are assertive, you foster positive relationships. The worksheet at the end of this chapter includes a section to help you apply mindfulness, enabling you to be more assertive.

SETTING HEALTHY BOUNDARIES

Healthy boundaries help us thrive while being assertive. Informing those around you how to care for you, connect with you, and treat you in a caring, gratifying, and safe way is one way to set boundaries.

While we black women are often expected to do, offer and sacrifice more at the expense of our mental and emotional health, you must understand that we all have a finite amount of energy, time, and resources.

Sadly, most of us fail to set healthy boundaries. Instead, we give ourselves away and waste our energy daily through several unfulfilling activities without realizing it. We fail to see that these activities drain and keep us from spending time on things that truly matter.

Here are four steps you can follow to set healthy boundaries:

- **Reframe and define:** Think of the pain and adverse effects you experience when people consistently violate your set boundaries. Then, write down the things, words, actions, and experiences that prevent you from feeling safe.
- **Communicate:** The next step is to tell those around you that you don't like those things you wrote down. Here are a few examples:

"I don't like it when you yell at me. It made me feel small."
"Please, don't do that to me again."
"I don't feel safe with you when you become aggressive. So I would appreciate it if we could talk about our differences rather than fight."

With these illustrations, you can set limits without blaming someone and focus on how it affects you when your boundaries are violated. But be aware that there will be those who may feel offended or attacked. You must understand that they are entitled to their opinions and feelings just as you are, so do not compromise yours for theirs to make them feel better.

- **Maintain boundaries:** Maintain your boundaries by upholding them when necessary, remembering who you've established boundaries with in the past, and remaining honest about those boundaries.
- **Be prepared to set consequences for those who violate your boundaries:** Be ready to talk about the repercussions of crossing your limits; here are some instances:

  "I won't give you my [time/friendship/advice/etc.] if you can't respect my boundaries."
  "I believe I made it clear that you had to respect my boundaries [state boundaries]. I need some space from you [specify a time limit or say you are unsure of how long you will need space for]."
  "We talked about [state the boundaries], but I don't feel like you respect me, so [convey the consequence]."

Remember that setting healthy boundaries protects you from harm and gives you the freedom to pay more attention to yourself.

SAYING NO THE RIGHT WAY

We must examine the reasons we struggle to express ourselves. Each of us has a distinct explanation, depending on our upbringing and personal characteristics.

So that you don't get accused of being the "angry black woman" or fall into the passiveness trap, you should follow these five steps to learn to say no and express yourself without feeling guilty:

- **Say no for the right reasons:** It's crucial to strike a healthy balance between the things you say yes to and the ones you decline. Saying no to requests that aren't one of your priorities becomes the ideal justification for your decision when you sort out your priorities.
- **Say it at the right time:** It is preferable to make a reasonable commitment within your means and to keep your word. When unsure of a situation, give yourself some time to consider your options.
- **Focus on body language and tone:** It's crucial to say no with a firm but calm voice, or you might sound rude. Consider adding a brief sentence explaining why you are saying no, and be aware of your demeanor. Additionally, avoid using a tone that treats the other person condescendingly.
- **Follow through:** No matter how adamant the other person is, if you disagree with the justification, stick to your choice. One caveat will convince others that your no can't be negotiated.

- **Be prepared and practice:** Learning to say no requires practice and experience before it becomes a natural part of you, just like any other life skill. So put it to use whenever you can, not only while making essential choices.

Here are a few creative ways to say no to encourage you in your newfound skill:

"Thanks, but I'll have to pass on that."
"I appreciate you asking me, but my time is already committed."
"I wish I could help you, but I'm too busy right now."
"I promised my coach (therapist, etc.) that I wouldn't accept any new projects at this time."
"I'm trying to live a more balanced life, so I'll have to decline."
"I appreciate the invitation, but my son has a soccer game that day, and I can't miss it."
"Simply put, I'm too busy right now. But I can recommend someone who might be able to assist you."
"Let me think about it. I'll get back to you."

Trust me, the more you say no to certain requests, the lighter and freer you'll feel, and the easier it will become to set clear, healthier boundaries in all aspects of your life.

SELF-CARE ASSESSMENT EXERCISE III

- Start by scheduling at least a fifteen-minute break to further explore this topic. Then, record any additional ideas or thoughts that come up in your journal and share your answers with a friend or your partner.
- Identify situations where you were either passive or aggressive. For example, it could be when your mother told you that you couldn't do anything right, and you didn't defend yourself or tell her how those words affected you.
- Identify how you can be assertive rather than passive or aggressive in a situation. For example, maybe your boss asks you to work late one day while others close for the day, but you've got plans for the night. Write down how you would respond assertively.
- Next, write down your top six life priorities based on how much of your time, energy, and resources they take.
- Reflect on this list, then create a new list based on how you would like to spend your time, energy, and resources on them in the next three months.
- I recommend you update this list every three months as your experience changes in your life. Write down any new life priorities you get during the next ninety days.
- Take a moment to consider your list of priorities and ask yourself, "Can I afford to do this, or would the additional burden be too overwhelming for my well-being and that of my family?"

Remember, you always have a choice. Additionally, you should exercise caution before committing to low-priority tasks if you are an active parent with a busy life and kids who demand a lot of energy.

We have spent time working on the mental and emotional aspect of self-care. Now, it's time to move on to the crucial physical elements of self-care. Enough of you to share includes your energy, and how you treat your body directly impacts your energy and confidence.

KEY POINTS

- You have a choice, and now is the time to put your life in order, define boundaries, and learn to say no to bad choices that will only deter you.
- The connection between emotions and illnesses stems from how we process and cope with emotions and, sometimes, how we avoid them.
- Assertiveness is taking a stand and calmly expressing yourself without attacking the other person.
- Healthy boundaries help us thrive while being assertive.
- The more you say no to certain requests, the lighter and freer you'll feel, and the easier it will become to set clear, healthier boundaries in all aspects of your life.

6

THE PHYSICAL SIDE OF
SELF-CARE

"Caring for myself is not self-indulgence; it is self-preservation, and that is an act of political warfare."

— AUDRE LORDE

Michelle and her three-year-old son, David, attended a birthday party for James, David's friend. Several moms, their kids, and I sat outside in the family's large, tree-covered backyard, eating pizza on blankets, and talking about the lack of support many black women felt in our lives.

Michelle's friend, Annalise, who grew up in Illinois, had recently returned from an extended stay in her native state with her two-year-old. I watched and listened as Annalise shared a story with Michelle about her visit to an emergency department in a hospital a few years ago.

Annalise had been suffering from a terrible illness. Unfortunately, not only did the emergency department staff not give her something for the pain, but they treated her like she was trying to trick or manipulate them into giving her painkillers. They didn't even acknowledge her or offer any assistance.

Meanwhile, there was nothing in Annalise's medical history to suggest she abused painkillers. She was a middle-aged woman and a good-natured Christian who had never experienced or struggled with substance misuse. She eventually found a diagnosis and the proper treatment elsewhere, but she was convinced that the former emergency room mistreated her because she was black.

Another woman, Crystal, also recounted her experience of how she kept putting off her doctor's and dentist's appointments because of the discrimination she had felt in the past.

And both Annalise and Crystal were probably right. It is commonly known that blacks and other minority groups in the U.S. suffer from more illnesses, have worse results, and die younger than white people. These health disparities were first documented back in the 1980s. Although a concerted effort by government agencies led to some progress, the most recent report in 2022 reveals continued gaps in race and ethnicity for all indicators.

According to Marian MacDorman, a researcher at the Maryland Population Research Center (MPRC) at the University of Maryland, black women are five times more likely to die from pregnancy-related cardiomyopathy and blood pressure disorders than white women. In fact, before COVID-19, black women were usually excluded from clinical trials and research studies on endometriosis.

Recognizing that racism and discrimination are deeply ingrained in our society's social, political, and economic structures, we must take our physical health into our hands, and self-care makes all the difference. Moreover, as black and white women are physically different, black women need a self-care routine that's tailored to them.

Therefore, this chapter will look at ways to create a personalized physical well-being plan depending on what you hope to achieve, whether you want to lose weight, improve your skincare, or learn to love your body. You will also find an exercise at the end of this chapter, which you can complete and use to gain more insight into where to start with your physical self-care routine.

ASSESSING YOUR PHYSICAL NEEDS

So far, we have looked at how you can make self-care a natural part of your life by working on your mental and emotional health. Equally important is meeting your physical needs because, as you may have realized, you have a unique set of them. You may want to manage specific health symptoms, eat healthily, lose weight, or tone up. Of course, there is an overlap between the emotional and physical sides of self-care.

For example, you may crave a cup of tea because it allows you a ten-minute rest and social time during a busy day and makes you feel cared for. However, suppose you are a regular tea-drinker. In that case, you might be addicted to caffeine (the main stimulant in tea), which you only notice when you don't drink as much as usual and perhaps suffer withdrawal symptoms such as headaches, tiredness, and nausea.

It could be that your schedule best fits in a morning workout, but because you can't say no, you have no time for yourself to unwind.

You may also have too many responsibilities that drain you emotionally to make time for physical activity, leading to weight gain and even lower confidence.

Sisters, we no longer see illness as a purely physical phenomenon, and the belief that a healthy mind leads to a healthy body has never been so prevalent.

So ask yourself the following questions:

"What are my physical needs?"
"What do I struggle with, feel hopeless about, feel powerless to change physically?"

Remember that one of the keys to cultivating the habit of taking care of your self-care needs is to meet your physical needs; rather than try to fill your frozen needs, you want to assess your physical needs and jot them down in your journal. You will find more details on how to get on with it in the Self-Care Assessment Exercise section of this chapter.

Do you currently meet your physical needs? Or are you waiting for the right time to start?

Perhaps you feel that you don't know enough to begin.

You will not be able to complete your self-care routine until you pay some attention to this area of your life. Doing so might bring up feelings, in which case, refer back to Chapters 3 through 5 for ways to release those feelings. That way, you stay in charge and increase your empowerment.

WHY YOUR DIET MIGHT NOT BE WORKING

Yes, curves are great; they are beautiful too! But they aren't so beautiful that you should try to get them at the expense of your health. You can be proud of your body and everything that comes with it, but if you are obese or overweight, there can be severe knock-on effects.

Before we continue, I must clarify that black women's bodies aren't the same as white women. Studies have shown that the same diet and exercise plan that makes white women lose 24 pounds makes black women lose 16 pounds. And this is because black women have lower energy requirements.

Here are some troubling physical health statistics about us black women:

- According to several studies, 5.8% of white women and 7.6% of black women suffer from heart disease.
- Approximately 46 out of every 100,000 black women died from strokes in 2016, compared to 35 out of every 100,000 white women.
- According to CDC data from 1980 to 2014, the diagnostic rate for diabetes in white women is 5.4 per 100, whereas it is 9.9 per 100 in black women, which is almost twice as high.

Black Americans are known to have the highest global prevalence of high blood pressure.

According to the U.S. Office of Minority Health, four out of every five African American women are overweight. In fact, compared to other populations in the U.S., African American women have the highest rates of obesity. This can lead to several health problems, from high blood pressure (hypertension) to heart disease and stroke. Black women don't just add weight; they put on extra pounds years before their white counterparts.

So to lose the same amount of weight, we have to do things differently from white women. According to researchers at the University of Pittsburgh School of Medicine, black women may need to eat fewer calories, approximately 150 less per day, or burn more than their Caucasian counterparts to lose a comparable amount of weight. But, of course, this was based on the women in the study; each woman will need a different caloric intake.

In addition, discrimination against black women poses health hazards, including medical professionals who don't take their concerns seriously and the lack of health education available to us. For instance, I have seen tons of calorie intake calculators for men and women, but none consider race.

While many different types of inequality affect people of color, racial health disparities are among the most pronounced and hard to change. These disparities are made worse by the fact that Black women make up the majority of healthcare employees, which is particularly upsetting and ironic. This unpleasant truth has become even more apparent due to the COVID-19 outbreak.

So what can you do to make your diet work?

It's simple! Treat yourself well by paying attention to your diet. Remember, you are what you eat. Fortunately, our ancestors brought many exquisite culinary customs to the southern states of the United States, South America, and the Caribbean. However, many of these culinary customs have been lost due to the impact of modern American eating patterns over the years.

Here are some tips for the perfect diet according to our ancestors:

- **Make rice and beans a regular meal:** The high-fiber dish of rice and beans is a global favorite. Add millet, sorghum, and teff, healthful grains of African ancestry, to your soups or combine them with peas.
- **Mashes and medleys are fun:** Yams and sweet potatoes can be baked or boiled, or they can be mashed along with eggplants, beans, grains, onions, and seasonings. One-pot cooking allows tastes to blend harmoniously! So mix some okra, corn, and tomatoes, or use purple cabbage and leeks to give your greens more color and flavor.
- **Make veggies the highlight of your meals:** Enjoy vegetables like okra, cabbage, green beans, or eggplant in more significant portions than the other components of your meal, whether steamed, sautéed, roasted, grilled, or raw.
- **Change your thinking about meat:** For flavor, use lean, healthy meats in fewer quantities. Ham-hocks can be swapped for smoked turkey or fish, or you can add lots of herbs and spices. You might not even realize that meat is present, thanks to the zingy flavors of African ancestry.
- **Spice up your food:** Low-sodium options to flavor grains, beans, vegetables, and shellfish include curries, peppers, coconut, fresh herbs, garlic, onions, and lemon. For a taste of African heritage, experiment with different spices each week.

- **Fruits for dessert:** At the end of your meal, you can add a pleasant flavor of contentment. Fruits like mangos, peaches, pineapples, berries, and other fresh or frozen fruits taste great, either simply or with a sprinkle of chopped almonds or coconut.
- **Drink enough fluids:** Water can become your favorite beverage with a bit of taste. To make reviving beverages like lemonade, mix crushed fruit or tiny amounts of 100% fruit juice with water or sparkling water. Another great substitute for soda and other heavily sweetened beverages is iced tea with a touch of honey.

Decide to change your eating habits. If you are following a calorie-counting diet, you should reduce the number of calories to see a change in your weight. Of course, you can find these foods everywhere, so eat them regularly and generously to nourish yourself.

You probably never learned to do this for various reasons, but we deserve to live healthy lives. So learn to eat a balanced diet and make a timetable for each day, outlining what, when, and how much you will eat.

HOW HARD AND OFTEN SHOULD WE EXERCISE?

As we know, exercise is essential to boosting our energy and immune system. Even if you've been a sloth until now, you can still attain fitness gradually, so do not rush the process in the beginning. Instead, choose an exercise plan that fits your life rather than dominates it.

Here are some general guidelines that might be helpful for the black woman when working out what exercise to take up:

- **Be realistic:** First, you must let go of those impossible beauty standards in our present-day social media. Instead, work out an exercise plan that suits your time, age, budget, lifestyle, social life, fitness levels, and your body's needs. Don't make exercise a strain or pain.
- **Start small:** I recommend you get 150 minutes of a moderate-intensity workout such as brisk walking or swimming, along with two sessions per week of muscle strengthening. But this will also depend on what your physical self-care plan involves. To tone up, you may need to increase your muscle strengthening; to lose weight, you may need more intense activities. The important thing is to find your journey.
- **Be gentle on yourself:** Use exercise as a way of pleasuring yourself, so always carry fragrant hair shampoo and body lotion when going to the gym. Pamper yourself; you should feel nurtured, pleasantly tingly, and relaxed afterward. Exercise is supposed to be a treat, a way of stretching and toning yourself, not a spartan punishment you must endure.
- **Exercise every week:**

  ○ Take the stairs instead of using the elevator.
  ○ Walk to the supermarket instead of driving down there.
  ○ Write in your diary when you are swimming, walking

your dog in the park, or meeting a friend for a game of squash.

That way, you will make exercise an essential part of your physical self-care.

If you are hurt emotionally, you will need to face what is happening at some point. Disappearing to the gym every time life gets tough is OK—up to a point—but if you never get to sort things out with people, face-to-face, then you could be missing out on the richness of human relationships and get stuck in your isolation. Exercise is an excellent way of meeting people.

In addition, you can network with new people if you're single by taking up a team sport, like volleyball, rather than swimming, walking, or jogging alone. Don't change and rush off afterward; wine and dine with other players. If you want to make friends, don't wait for someone else to make the first move. You could always take the initiative.

TIME TO RELAX AND RECHARGE

It is so easy to say we want to relax and recharge our batteries, yet it can be so hard to do so. Furthermore, what you usually think of as relaxation might not often be ideal. For instance, you might watch TV until your eyes get swollen. You might also go on a spending spree or drive your car down a highway at high speed to release tension.

Of course, there is nothing wrong with these activities (unless they put you and others in grave danger). Still, there is something wrong when your ONLY means of relaxation involves stressful activities.

Although there is no perfect formula for black women to find the time to relax and recharge, here are some suggestions:

- **Sip and eat your way to relaxation:** You can sip some green tea which gives you the benefits of L-theanine, a chemical that can help reduce the body's stress responses. You can also try to eat some chocolate, chew some gum, or go tropical and eat some juicy mangoes. Mangoes contain linalool, which helps to reduce stress and anxiety.
- **Find inner peace:** Find some quiet time to meditate and connect with your true self. You can also try breathing exercises such as breathing slow and fast to calm your nerves.
- **Treat your body uniquely:** Get your favorite oils or cream, rub them into your palms, and massage every part of your body, from your joints and the space between your fingers to your scalp. Tug your hair out gently and massage every area underneath. You can also try acupressure to help relieve stress and anxiety.
- **Make space for yourself:** Find some time to be alone in your element. For instance, you could have a hot bath with scented candles or just sit and stare out the window. You could also stop and sniff those flowers with beautiful scents. Keep a fresh jar of your preferred

kind in the living room or close to your desk so you
may take a sniff whenever you feel stressed.

Binging on some YouTube videos can also help you relax and
recharge. Indeed, laughter is the best mood elevator to relieve
stress. Even science agrees that laughter is the best medicine, so
explore those funny videos and photos online.

GET QUALITY SLEEP

There is no better healer than sleep, as it allows our body to
repair itself and our mind to sift through experiences in the
form of dreams. Some people fall asleep once their heads hit the
pillow, while others toss and turn for hours.

You might need to experiment to get your physical needs met
for sleep. For instance, do you respond well to naps in the
middle of the day? Do you need to sleep in total darkness? Or
do you need earplugs for complete silence?

How many hours of sleep do you need on average? Women
generally need less sleep as they age, but we vary greatly. Also,
going through emotional upheavals, such as grief, relocation,
changing your job, or being in therapy, will probably make you
tired. Sometimes, you can feel exhausted even though you slept
for ten hours. Other times, you can feel refreshed after sleeping
for only four hours. Exercise and diet also directly impact the
quality of your sleep.

That said, here are some helpful hints to help you sleep better:

- **Get in sync with your natural sleep-wake cycle (also known as circadian rhythm):** You can do this by trying to be consistent with what time you sleep and wake up every day. You should limit your napping if you have trouble falling asleep.
- **Control your exposure to light:** Our body produces melatonin, a hormone that helps control our sleep-wake cycle, and is regulated by exposure to sunlight. Our brain releases more melatonin in the dark, which makes us sleepy, and less in the light, which makes us more awake.
- **Release some emotions:** You could cry, yawn, or talk on the phone to someone about what's bothering you. Whatever you do, get those feelings off your chest. Also, try to ensure that your environment is quiet when you want to process and release your emotions. If you're in a busy place, you can put on some earplugs.

If you practice these tips, you'll feel much more refreshed and energized than before. Remember to exercise often and eat healthy, as your daytime eating habits also affect how well you sleep. Avoid eating late at night, especially close to bedtime.

SELF-CARE ASSESSMENT EXERCISE IV

In this exercise, you'll create a physical activity tracker to enable you to understand better what you need to work on.

- At the end of the week, write down the exercises you did each day, their duration, intensity, and effects.
- Write the meals you ate every day of the week— breakfasts, lunches, and dinners. Remember to add the snacks and desserts you ate and how many glasses of water you drank.
- Write down how many hours you slept each day of the week.
- Make a list of the things you did to unwind and recharge.

Take a look at your answers and work on how you can move closer to achieving the physical needs of your self-care goals the following week. Then, repeat this exercise until you see yourself improve and get better.

Part of the physical self-care exercises is to ensure that you do not miss any of your appointments. As your self-care and self-love improve, the exercises will become easier. Always remember that the best way to stand up to injustice is to be proud to put yourself first. The next step is to work on our goals and dreams and create a plan to achieve them.

KEY POINTS

- You must take your physical health into your hands, and self-care makes all the difference.
- One of the keys to cultivating the habit of taking care of your self-care needs is to meet your physical needs; rather than try to fill your frozen needs, you want to assess your physical needs and jot them down in your journal.
- Treat yourself well by paying attention to your diet. Remember, you are what you eat.
- Exercise is essential to boost your energy and immune system.
- There is no better healer than sleep, as it allows our body to repair itself and our mind to sift through experiences in the form of dreams.

7

STRIVING FOR WHAT YOU DESERVE

"Self-worth cannot be verified by others. You are worthy because you say it is so. If you depend on others for your value, it is other-worth."

— WAYNE W. DYER

I have heard many stories of black women who don't have much athletic training find superhuman strength to rescue children, spouses, or friends in desperate situations. They find this strength when the lives of their loved ones are threatened, but how is this even possible when others see us as the weaker gender?

Of course, it has to do with a sense of worth. For example, when we come in contact with people who possess admirable qualities that we love and value, we are always ready and willing to protect their interests. We also tend to invest our mental, emotional, and physical energies to ensure they are safe and well. As black women, we are encouraged and socially rewarded for looking after others.

Even the idea of making ourselves pretty is so that we can greatly appeal to those around us, get a job, or be famous. Why not take care of ourselves, make ourselves attractive for *our* pleasure, and then, if we choose, extend that pleasure to others?

Perhaps we fear that this kind of attention to ourselves would mean we are selfish and egotistical. Again, this fear stems from our concern for other people, especially people of different races, rather than ourselves—an extended form of our social conditioning.

Dyer's quote at the beginning of this chapter reminds us that being worthy means depending on yourself for your true value. It's easy for a white man with a doctorate degree to preach about self-worth and emphasize the need to give credit where credit is due. Nevertheless, always remember that your opinion of yourself matters more than anyone else's.

So we will start this chapter with an understanding of self-worth and why it's essential to appreciate your true value to see that you are worthy of so much more. We all have immense value, and there is power in knowing this. Learning about your true worth will push you to use the ability to strive for what you want.

WHAT IS SELF-WORTH AND HOW TO APPRECIATE YOURS

The journey I began by writing this book earned me visitation rights into the hearts and minds of hundreds of incredible black women worldwide. I found that questions about our worth loom large: are we generally considered as worthy as women from other races? Is everything just peachy as far as we're concerned?

Have we as a race achieved our long-sought-for equality, or do we still tend to struggle with our world to acknowledge our substance or value? Are we given the respect and attention we deserve?

Although these questions aren't new, the answers aren't easy either. It seems that we black women continue to face the challenge of expressing and accessing a sense of self-esteem, and the answers to questions such as "How do you define your worth?" are nuanced by time, place, and culture.

After trying to answer these questions for myself, I realized that the actual definition of "self-worth" is centered around how much we value ourselves. Thus, we couldn't talk about self-love without talking about the following terms:

- **Conditions of worth:** the do's and don'ts that you live by to feel appreciated and accepted by others.
- **Self-esteem:** the honor, value, and worth you place on yourself.

- **Self-confidence:** how you accept and trust yourself to have a sense of control in your life.
- **Self-concept:** your ordered set of thoughts and views about yourself.
- **Self-compassion:** how kind and compassionate are you to yourself when you struggle, falter, or feel unworthy, as opposed to disregarding your suffering or torturing yourself with self-criticism?

When our black female friend needs support, we usually remind her about how amazing she is. To discover our self-worth, we must treat ourselves with this same compassion. We are black! We are beautiful!! We are amazing!!!

If the virtue of modesty pulls your self-image toward the ground, the value of self-worth raises it toward the sky. The idea behind self-worth is to make as high an appraisal of yourself as possible. It is an abiding belief in what you are made of deep down as a black woman.

Wisdom in action is forgetting what others think, even if they are critical of you. Would past and present legends have attempted or succeeded in their visions and goals if they defeated themselves because of faltering self-worth?

Therefore, we must find more of our self-worth and learn to appreciate it. Knowing your true value will make your life worth living and bring an array of opportunities within your grasp.

To appreciate your worth, value, and sense of fulfillment, you must first evaluate yourself honestly. Set aside some quiet time so that you can reflect in peace. You should ask yourself the following questions and write down the answers in your journal:

- What gives you joy?
- What contributions do you make?
- Do you feel acknowledged for these contributions?
- Do you nurture and enjoy your relationships?
- If yes, are your relationships fulfilling?
- What are your goals and dreams?
- Are the objectives you set for yourself being met?
- Do your lifestyle and activities help you feel good about yourself?

Consider the answers to these questions even if you don't wish to record them. And don't hesitate to add more questions centered on the details of your own life.

Assessing yourself and where you stand is vital to your ability to function freely as a black woman in today's world. Be original in how you evaluate yourself. Do you think this is silly? Well, it isn't. If anything, it's only a happy acceptance of who you are. You validate yourself by assessing and acknowledging your skills, and you must be able to do so before anyone else can validate you. However, do not try to compare yourself with others; instead, stay in your lane. After all, your journey is different and unique to you.

YOU ARE WORTHY OF PERSONAL GROWTH

There was a time when I went about my daily business after waking up. Back then, I would prepare for the day's work after making breakfast. Usually, I would go to the gym, hang out with my friends, and prepare dinner. And after reading and making plans for the next day, I would go to bed. I repeated this routine every day. But as the COVID-19 pandemic worsened, things began to feel like a vicious monotony. So I started to feel drained.

It's like that with many black women. At some point, it starts to feel like our dreams and goals are buried in thick molasses in our heads. And even as we make our way through this new normal, we could still feel "stuck."

The good news is that you can seek personal growth and development assistance. I've been on a personal development journey for quite some time, so I am familiar with the experience. Everybody's journey to personal improvement is different, so it's only natural that everyone's development would be unique.

Focus your attention on things that contribute to your growth and personal development. Your self-awareness, self-esteem, skill set, and aspirations are all increased through personal development. The truth is, personal development encompasses far more than just personal growth or career advancement. It covers all areas of your life where you'd like to improve, and it doesn't distinguish how it manifests for you. The great thing about personal development is that it is linked to similar, if not the same, areas of self-care.

Below, I've included five main avenues for personal growth. You'll realize as you read them that you've already begun working on your personal development:

- **Mental:** Fitness and brain exercise are essential for personal development. The mind can be developed through workshops, training sessions, or rest. Rest is just as important, if not more so, than a mental exercise. Additionally, as your level of mental fitness grows, so will your ability to adapt, be creative, and be aware of yourself.
- **Social:** All forms of personal development require social relationships and interactions. After all, self-improvement is a collaborative undertaking. Humans need a social connection to grow and learn since we are social beings. Through our social interactions, we also learn vital skills, including the ability to collaborate, solve problems, form connections, and provide feedback. We can also learn from those around us and their experiences.
- **Spiritual:** Spirituality can foster personal development whether or not you're religious. However, it's important to realize that religion and spirituality are two separate ideas. Spirituality here implies a deeper awareness of who you are and the world around you. So it will help you explore yourself and your values.

- **Emotional:** Emotional personal growth and emotional intelligence frequently go hand in hand. Understanding emotions is the most basic form of emotional intelligence, and a wide range of events can facilitate the development of your emotional self. You likely encouraged emotional growth along the way if you reflect on your journey and notice your growth. Understanding the part your emotions and thoughts played during this journey requires emotional intelligence.

- **Physical:** A sound body feeds a sound mind. Your mental, emotional, and physical health are all interdependent. The key conversation theme in this area of personal development is physical health, which includes diet, rest, exercise, and movement. It's likely that by attending to your physical requirements, your mental health will also advance. We already talked about ways you can build this area of personal development in Chapter 6, so feel free to check it out.

As a black woman, you must learn how to present yourself to the world. Luckily, you don't have to struggle so hard with everything we have covered. It took me some time to discover this, but conventional personal development has never truly benefited me. Famous gurus have always inspired me, but I've only ever taken advice to heart when it's from people I can relate to—leaders who speak my language and understand my culture. They set the example for how I want to present myself to the world as a black woman because they are fearless and successful.

DREAMS AND GOALS THAT YOU DESERVE

It seems odd that adults often don't know what they want and often don't hold the power to act on their dreams. Yet, that's the norm. Kids, however, seem to know exactly what they want. Why? One reason is that they have the time to daydream, fantasize, and think. Many black women don't take the time to daydream or think about what they would love to do.

If you haven't asked yourself lately what you want, you probably don't know the answer. You are either living out someone else's dreams, or you are settling for what's simply good when you could have what is best. Both cases lead to an unfulfilled life, feelings of resentment, and the inevitable question: "Is this all there is to life?"

Have you ever taken the time to think about what your dream life is? What career would you rather have? What goals have you set for your life? What does your ideal day look like?

I have kept a journal and vision board for over ten years. In both of these, I write about (and even post pictures of) my dream life. The most amazing part about my vision board and dream journal have been watching myself gradually bring my dreams to life. I often look back at the dreams I set ten years ago and think, "*Wow, I actually did that!*" So many of the things I've written down are now a reality!

There is so much power in deciding what you want. Clarity gives you energy. When you know what you want and begin acting on it (even in small ways), every day of your life will become more exciting. If you were to look back at your life so far, you would see unfolding miracles that made your life events. You were given what you needed when you needed it, usually not before. Every event in your life moves you a bit closer to your destination. There is a process going on in your life.

No matter your age, think of yourself as the director and producer of your life rather than the adjunct player in someone else's. Own your place in the world, and consider what would be good for you for a change.

When you own your worth, you honor women everywhere in many ways, and the trickle-down effect of your actions will ultimately reach all parts of the world. Here is a simple three-step process I recommend for every black woman to help her identify her dreams and goals:

- Create a list of about twenty to thirty things you strongly desire. This could be related to your family, health, finances, or work life. No idea is too stupid or too big.
- Next, look at your list and pick the top five items that are most important to you. This might be hard, but it is essential that these five dreams are highly significant to you.
- (Tip: If you found out you want a house with a pool, even if it's just a garden space for a paddling pool, it's possibly because you envision yourself taking ten minutes to unwind, not because the kids will love it. And that's a bonus.)

- Finally, create two new lists in your journal. The first list is for the top five things you picked, and the second is for the remaining items.

That's it! You have just identified the five most essential things you deserve. The most important part of choosing and setting goals is ensuring they are yours. To live your life fully, you must be confident in designing your goals and aligning them with your values and passions. Please, be true to yourself and know what is good enough for you. This exercise is not about setting goals so you can meet others' expectations. It is about your dreams, as they are aligned with YOUR passions. After all, you will never know if something will work until you try it.

The next step is working on the first list with your top five items. The second list automatically becomes the one you must avoid at all costs. Looking at the second list will give you an idea of the things you should avoid.

When you're not aware of your dreams and goals, you might lose sight of your choices. But when you overcome the urge to accept what society dictates, you'll experience an enormous sense of freedom. You have options in life, but you need to be willing to chase them.

CREATING STEPS TO ACHIEVE YOUR DREAMS AND GOALS

You are in charge of your life, so you can create the life you desire. We sometimes make the life we believe we desire, which meets many of our ideals but doesn't make us happy. Our happiness and fulfillment will only feel complete when we connect to what we genuinely want and live out our passions.

The things we want and strive for are often not connected to our true selves, which is why we achieve them and still feel empty and unfulfilled. So we must define what we want based on whether they align with our core. Again, your focus should be on the five things you highlighted on the first list in the previous section.

Reaching for these ideals may also be looked upon as striving for excellence. A few things come to mind when exploring this process. What I do recommend is starting with the end in mind. Knowing where you want to be and what you want to achieve, then acting on this vision will help you become more focused and make your dreams achievable in the long run.

Once you are ready, here are seven steps every black woman can take to turn her dreams and goals into reality:

- **Be open-minded:** You must maintain an open mind and accept whatever obstacles you encounter with gratitude if you want to achieve the life of your dreams. Everybody dreams, and as unique as our dreams are, they are often alike. So sharing your dreams can be quite beneficial. Naturally, people want to assist others, especially if they can relate to their ideas. So all you have to do is allow them to participate.
- **Create actionable plans:** Making plans provides you with direction and a clear idea of the actions you need to take to achieve your dreams. You should never rely

on fate to bring your dreams to life if you want to be an achiever. Instead, you should grow and move forward every day. Even if you're progressing slowly, it is still better than procrastinating or being complacent.

- **Find motivation:** Sometimes, external circumstances force us to give up on our goals and look for alternatives, no matter how long we have had a dream and how strongly we want it to come true. So look for inspiration to keep your dream alive and attainable.

Indeed, you are surrounded by a lot of successful people. But don't let that discourage you into thinking they are too intelligent and successful to interact with you. Make an effort to get along with them. These diligent professionals are never short on advice, so learning from their lifestyle alone is an effective way to know what to do to achieve your goals.

- **Seek out opportunities:** You can't succeed if you don't try. You should always take advantage of new possibilities, enjoy traveling, look forward to meeting new people, communicate, and learn.
- **Listen to your instincts:** Listen to and trust your instincts, but do not rely on them alone. Be true to yourself and stick to your principles. Many people will try to discourage you from pursuing your goals by telling you they are unattainable. Additionally, there will be times when you will consider giving up. But don't allow these thoughts to control you. You need to be resilient. If you have a plan, you'll have a road map

that will take you safely through the hurdles and obstacle-filled forests.

- **Don't be afraid:** Fear is a powerful feeling that could seriously impede your progress. But once you get through it, you'll realize nothing is impossible. Everyone who has mustered the resolve to pursue their aspirations initially felt frightened. Even many of the top achievers you see today struggled with fear at some point. It's okay to be afraid. Uncertainty terrifies me, too. But that is the examination everyone who dares to pursue their aspirations must pass.

- **Know that it's okay to fail:** Every success story begins with setbacks and bad luck, so don't be afraid of failing. You must develop this mindset before setting out on your journey. You gain new knowledge, develop, and get stronger when you fail. You also grow closer to living the life of your dreams with each failure. When we reach our goals and dreams, there is always more to take their place. Even if you don't make it the first time, you will eventually make it if you never give up. Every single step of progress needs to be acknowledged and celebrated. Thus, you must always strive to develop a growth mindset.

As we wrap up this chapter, I want to leave you with these wise words from Nelson Mandela: "Vision without action is just a dream, action without vision just passes the time, and vision with action can change the world." This means that you should find your vision and create action to see your dreams and goals become a reality.

Finally, when you achieve your goals and dreams, don't forget that you got what you wanted. Never get so bogged down with your goal's responsibility that you forget it is what you wanted!

SELF-CARE ASSESSMENT EXERCISE V

- Pick up the first list where you listed the five things you want. It's time to break down each item on the list into smaller achievable goals so you do not procrastinate. For example, let's say the five items on your list are

  - a personal goal;
  - a relationship goal;
  - a career goal;
  - a financial goal; and
  - a health goal.

- For each goal, identify short-term steps you will need to take to achieve it and a realistic timeframe. For example, you can have four short-term steps for the next four weeks—that is, one short-term step for each week.
- Again, your goals should be specific, measurable, and time-bound.

Having aligned your goals with your passions, it is time we move on to examining factors that can hinder you. Perhaps, you have some obstacles that prevent you from achieving your goals and dreams. In the next chapter, you will be able to determine what stops you and the solutions to overcoming those obstacles. Throughout these chapters, the word confidence has been kept to a minimum; but it is the glue that will piece together our self-care practices and ensure that this new habit becomes the norm, just like happiness!

KEY POINTS

- The idea behind self-worth is to make as high an appraisal of yourself as possible.
- Knowing your true value will make your life worth living and bring an array of opportunities within your grasp.
- There is so much power in deciding what you want. Clarity gives you energy. When you know what you want and begin acting on it (even in small ways), every day of your life will become more exciting.
- Our happiness and fulfillment will only feel complete when we connect to what we genuinely want and live out our passions.

8

FINDING YOUR BLACK MAGIC CONFIDENCE

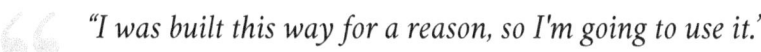 *"I was built this way for a reason, so I'm going to use it."*

— SIMONE BILES

L et's take a step back to something even more fundamental. Sometimes, the essential ingredient for real improvement is neglected in our eager efforts to improve. And that is a deep and meaningful realization of our black magic— in other words, our self-confidence. One annoying aspect of most forms of adversity and setback is that they chip away at your self-confidence.

Self-confidence is the black woman's superpower. The moment you start to believe in yourself, the magic starts happening. So far, all the subjects we have discussed should positively impact your confidence. But we all know there is a difference between confidence and that unique feeling that we are privileged to be able to experience black magic confidence.

Once, my friend Jackie shared with me how someone faked her confidence when needed, but it still wasn't enough.

Jackie had gone to Bartram's Garden, and directly in front of her was Rachel, a big black woman wearing a large, wide hat and carrying a fan. It was a hot evening, and the atmosphere wasn't all that friendly. The meeting finally got to the part where people were invited to stand up and tell the gathering a story from their lives.

Rachel stood up and started talking to everyone in the gathering. Few people paid attention to what she was saying when suddenly, she started yelling, "Oh, Yea! Thank you! Thank you for having me share my feelings in my darkest hour!"

Before Jackie knew what was happening, Rachel started jumping up and down, flailing her very ample arms around in the air while waving her fan like she was trying to chase away imaginary flies. This continued for what seemed like a lifetime. She continued to jump and dance and spin around as she yelled her thanks.

Then, after reaching a point of total exhaustion, she hurled herself backward and almost fell on Jackie. Panicked and fearing for her life, Jackie quickly jumped and ran down to a safer spot, laughing all the way.

After everything had calmed down, Jackie decided to approach Rachel to know precisely what had happened. It turned out that the 43-year-old author had felt insecure among strangers, so she thought the best way forward was to fake her confidence. According to Jackie, Rachel tried to project a persona that was cool, sardonic, and funny so people would accept her. However, Rachel felt this may have backfired, as her new acquaintances may not take her social anxiety seriously if she confided in them.

Rachel also added that her fake confidence usually keeps her from receiving the care she craves for and actually deserves. So Jackie scheduled a date for Rachel and I to meet and discuss this in detail. And when we met, I recommended some self-care practices and additional tips on building self-confidence rather than faking it. As we talked, Rachel soon felt better, and over time, she was able to build self-confidence.

So if you have been depressed or have had a setback recently, or you have some blocks that prevent you from achieving your set goals and the dreams you have highlighted, you may need to build your self-confidence.

Most people will recognize the superficial aspects of self-confidence. Specifically, it is easy to identify a person who appears self-confident, even though little is known about the inner aspects of self-confidence. This final chapter deals with valid, practical strategies for black women to develop, restore, or rebuild their self-confidence without feeling like they need to "fake it till they make it."

A CASE OF IMPOSTOR SYNDROME

No matter how well Rachel did, she always felt she wasn't good enough for the rarefied publishing world. She was a hardworking black woman who didn't come from a pedigree. She felt (and sometimes literally was) unacknowledged in the hallways, and her voice was hardly heard.

"It wasn't rare for me to propose ideas in meetings that were met with a cool welcome, but two meetings later, someone else offered a similar idea, and it was immediately hailed as a mustwrite narrative," Rachel had explained during our meeting.

Even though she knew she could do the work, she was riddled with doubt. Years later, she learned there was a term for what she felt: impostor syndrome.

Impostor syndrome is the view or feeling that you are an intellectual or professional fraud, and many black women struggle with this mindset. For instance, you have the training, qualifications, and abilities to perform a job but you may still be full of self-doubt—and not because you aren't seeing positive examples in your work.

Although you might not be able to perceive it, impostor syndrome is rampant in the office. Why do I feel like an impostor even though I'm eminently suited for this job? It is a sentiment that many individuals can relate to. Despite having formal education and training, many people have never been able to overcome self-doubt and advance to a greater degree of achievement.

Anyone can ask this question; however, impostor syndrome disproportionately impacts some groups more than others, such as women of color, particularly black women. Impostor syndrome develops when someone experiences systemic oppression and regularly hears that they are inferior or undeserving of achievement. Then they start to do things in a way that contradicts that narrative. Deciding to increase your confidence is the simplest method to overcome impostor feelings.

SELF-ESTEEM VS. SELF-CONFIDENCE

How does self-esteem differ from self-confidence, and how can understanding this difference ultimately change how we live? Or perhaps more fundamental than these questions: why is the topic of self-worth only superficially and usually interchangeably connected with self-esteem? And how could the inclusion of this difference enhance the self-improvement material that already colors our lives and conversations?

Perhaps the best way to explain the difference between self-esteem and self-confidence (or even explain what self-worth is in the first place) is to review my discovery process.

While self-esteem and self-confidence overlap, they are each unique. Self-esteem is the belief in your ineffable values, while self-confidence is the belief in your abilities.

Low self-confidence or low self-esteem is common among black women. Others may find it limiting or incapacitating, while some people are only affected in certain circumstances.

But if you lack confidence or self-esteem, you can discover that particular bad or disappointing situations impact how you view yourself. Negative expectations for the future might result in a self-reinforcing cycle of negative thoughts that discourage you from trying. This often leads to poor results.

For instance, if you don't feel confident and get a poor grade on an assignment, you might say, "What else was there to expect? I'm a moron. I'm not good enough, so I should quit now and save everyone the trouble."

However, if you have a positive self-perception and get a bad grade, you might say, "I made mistakes this time, but I'll improve so I can perform better next time." Even though the low grade may disappoint you, it doesn't make you feel less of a person. The common determinants of low self-esteem are as follows:

- Shyness
- Communication issues
- Social anxiety
- Lack of assertiveness

That critical solid inner voice that tends to speak out loudly when you feel upset, overwhelmed, or evaluated by others may develop from low self-esteem. This inner critic can significantly worsen one's emotional misery by fueling depressive, anxious, or irrational thoughts.

Because you don't feel deserving of it, you can't exercise self-care without self-esteem; thus, there is a strong relationship between the two that eventually results in confidence. We discover how much we are worth, how much we can do, and how much we can develop from happy and sad situations when we give ourselves the chance to practice self-care.

However, it is not a simple or quick procedure because it necessitates a great deal of compassion for ourselves. The first step in this process is learning to appreciate oneself and having a healthy sense of self-worth.

If we don't stop reflecting on what we do daily, we won't have time to value our efforts and love ourselves enough. Although there isn't a quick fix or magic solution for low self-esteem, there are steps we can take to boost our self-esteem and start appreciating ourselves for who we are. In the next section, you will discover ways to increase your self-confidence and self-esteem.

BECOMING INDEPENDENT

After all, the idea of becoming independent appeals to black women. We would all undoubtedly wish to claim our independence, ownership of our narratives, and the ability to raise our hands to celebrate our freedom.

But occasionally, it is simply not the case. We are dependent at times. Sometimes, we discover that we depend more on others than on ourselves. And to be honest, that's fine. We are not designed to handle everything independently since life occasionally throws us curveballs.

However, there is such a thing as excessively depending on other people. It's unwise to let someone else's aspirations, objectives, ideas, or feelings take precedence over yours, whether that person is your friend, relative, or partner. Over-dependence on another person can undermine your self-worth, delay your goals, and lead to you overlooking your own needs. And that's simply unacceptable.

You should take a step back and attempt to restore some of your freedom, and here's how to go about it:

- **Take action by yourself:** Are you unclear whether the email you just wrote might come off as casual or irrational? Refrain from showing it to your friend or anybody else nearby for comments. Instead, read it over before sending it. Although it may seem insignificant, exercising your right to freewill can significantly influence you.
- **Learn more about yourself:** If you feel like you've forgotten yourself a little bit later, you may need to stop putting all your attention and energy on someone else. It's time to assess your situation. Spend some time alone getting back in touch with the things you love. Make it a personal discipline that involves only you and no one else.
- **Concentrate on your best qualities:** Just so you know, you are great! You deserve to be here just as much as anyone else because you are black, have unique abilities, and a distinct viewpoint. I won't always be here to tell you that, though. So you must always remind yourself.

Now, take out your journal and list at least ten positive qualities you appreciate about yourself. When you are aware of your strengths, you will be more motivated to work hard to develop into a wonderful person.

- **Give yourself some emotional support:** True independence only becomes apparent when you discover that you can support yourself emotionally when you acknowledge that you have feelings and that you can soothe them.

So allow yourself to experience your emotions instead of dismissing them as unimportant. Experience them fully and give yourself time to discover what gives you comfort on your own. Keep in mind that you have the power to transform both your life and the world around you. Doing so will help you feel independent enough to scream, raise your hands, and wave at me.

PROVEN STRATEGIES TO FIND YOUR BLACK MAGIC CONFIDENCE

It's crucial to know how to display self-assurance outside the office. Gaining more self-assurance can make it easier for you to find a partner with whom you can have a fulfilling relationship. You might also look for new possibilities to promote personal growth and learn how to handle disagreements.

You must be willing to alter your state to learn how to increase your confidence. Your state is essentially how you are feeling at any given moment. How you think of yourself at that particular moment affects your mood. But the good news is that you can alter your condition at any time, regardless of what is happening around you.

The following exercises will help you master your emotions and help you become more confident. Although these exercises have been mentioned in previous chapters, I would still like to reiterate them here to help you build the confidence typical of black women:

- **Modifying your physiology:** The quickest confidence-boosting advice is to alter your physiology drastically. So hold a straight posture while taking deep breaths. And when you walk, take quick, deliberate steps to cover more ground. Maintaining this stance makes you feel more powerful, and your mind follows your body wherever it goes.
- **Take ownership of your accomplishments:** Self-assured people may earn more money at work for one simple reason: they own up to their successes and do so when it counts the most. It's not bragging to mention your contribution to your manager or CEO if it helped the organization achieve a goal or resulted in a beneficial outcome. It won't just make you appear excellent if you say it. In fact, it will also make you feel good.
- **Embrace gratitude:** Be grateful for each stage of the procedure. The secret to happiness is learning to be grateful. When you are thankful, abundance emerges, and fear vanishes. So kill the idea that your body exists

solely for you to look at, or worse, for others to gaze at. Your body is more than just a container or a work of art. Consider the many tasks your body accomplishes for you. Instead of focusing on what you lack, consider all the things you can be thankful for.

Use visualization techniques to create in your mind a clear image of realizing your utmost potential. See it, feel it, and it will manifest when you shift your perspective from one of negativity to one of abundance. Once we become adept at visualizing positively, we will achieve our goals and dreams much faster.

- **Change your perspective:** Sometimes, changing your perspective is all it takes to get yourself out of a slump. You must first alter the way you view failure. My best advice for boosting confidence is as follows:

  ○ Take failures as opportunities rather than barriers
  ○ Consider the positive rather than the bad
  ○ Accept all of life's gifts and live courageously

- **Try power poses:** Connecting with your inner strength is one of the most effective methods to boost your confidence. We all possess inner power, yet it can be challenging to remember this when we're down. To re-establish contact with your powerful core, think about creating your unique power stance and deep breathing.
- **Use the power of proximity:** You may boost your self-confidence by surrounding yourself with motivators

and supporters. Find people who will help you succeed in whatever you want to achieve in life. By leveraging the power of proximity, you will have a strong support system that will push you to improve while offering support.

- **Learn new skills:** Fear and anxiety are innate human emotions. However, when you have confidence in yourself, you understand that these feelings are there to motivate you to act, not to stop you. So you can learn new skills to overcome your fear and feelings of inadequacy.
- **Live in the present:** Forgiving and letting go of the past can be challenging. We seek to avoid suffering and satisfy our desire for certainty, but doing so keeps us from being present. Instead of fussing over the past or future, learn to enjoy what you have right now. When you're conscious of the present, your anxiety will reduce, and your confidence will grow.

The values in this chapter are some of the most relevant to our lives because every second of every waking minute is "looking through our own eyes" out onto the world. In other words, your feelings about yourself (self-confidence) and your appraisal of yourself (self-worth) color how you interact with others, make decisions and generally feel about life.

The black woman with higher levels of self-confidence is likely to be successful in her endeavors, have less stress, and be involved in more functional and rewarding relationships. We all know how it feels to doubt ourselves; even the most successful black women experience challenges in their love lives, and the most beautiful ones often worry about how they look (ask a black supermodel!).

To live wisely is to attempt to build self-esteem, even as an adult. Our parents and society laid the foundations for our senses of self. But now that we're adults, we must take responsibility for becoming the most confident black women we can be. Life is full of little moments of choice in which we can face anxiety and be pushed around by others to do things we would rather not do. But learning to live deliberately with confidence and knowing how to love ourselves by being consistently happy are fundamental to happiness and fulfillment. Indeed, it is much like oiling a noisy axle on an automobile; it takes time and energy to do it. But if we must travel the distance (life) with or without efficiency and quiet, why not make the journey as smooth and pleasant as possible?

KEY POINTS

- Self-confidence is the black woman's superpower.
- Impostor syndrome is the view or feeling that you are an intellectual or professional fraud, and many black women struggle with this mindset.
- While self-esteem and self-confidence overlap, they are each unique. Self-esteem is the belief in your ineffable values, while self-confidence is the belief in your abilities.

- Over-dependence on another person can undermine your self-worth, delay your goals, and lead to you overlooking your own needs.
- The black woman with higher levels of self-confidence is likely to be successful in her endeavors, have less stress, and be involved in more functional and rewarding relationships.

CONCLUSION

"You are your best thing."

— TONI MORRISON

As you have already learned, self-care is how you embrace and incorporate the care of the mind, body, and spirit into your being and daily life ritual. First, it starts on the inside (emotional, mental, and spiritual) and then proceeds to the outside (social, physical, practical, and professional).

Perhaps, you always hear a voice inside your head telling you that taking care of yourself is not for you. Or maybe the voice says that you have to be strong because the world is against you and counting on you to fail. Or that one day, the universe will send you somebody who will love you more than you love yourself.

Well, show me any supporting text that explicitly states that black women do not deserve the same level of love and tenderness bestowed upon women and men of other races and nationalities. I bet you will find none.

It is high time we stopped allowing other people's opinions of us to define us, but we have to work together and make a change. To live our life to its fullest potential, we must take care of ourselves in all aspects: emotionally, mentally, spiritually, physically, socially, practically, and professionally.

I know it's shameful that we have to deal with racism in these so-called advanced times. It's bad enough that racism affects every part of our lives, from our finances to our health. It's embarrassing that a black woman may feel scared talking to her doctor or even walking down the street. But this disgust, shame, and embarrassment aren't on us—that's on society! And, of course, we should be protesting this, but now is the time to find an even louder voice, the power of confidence and happiness.

Self-care, especially for black women, is a revolutionary act whose time has come. It is not a race-based privilege. Take a look at 23-year-old Naomi Osaka, who is now shaking up the world of Tennis. She took a stand when she withdrew from the Cincinnati Masters in a demonstration against the police shooting of Jacob Blake, causing organizers to postpone the match for a day.

Osaka, via social media, withdrew from the Grand Slam competitions in May 2021. She explained that she "never wanted to be a distraction" and had been struggling with "long bouts of depression" since 2018. Despite her mental illness and boos from the audience, she fought and defeated Serena Williams in the U.S. Open that same year.

Osaka's defiance had an immediate effect since she was willing to talk openly and process her emotions in front of others in real-time. She also received a flood of support from prominent athletes, celebrities, and members of the general public.

"After I disclosed my troubles . . . [m]any athletes I met with admitted that they had also been suffering in silence," claims Osaka. Soon, athletes like golfer Mariah Stackhouse, swimmer Simone Manuel, and gymnast Simone Biles began to speak out about the adverse effects of competitive sports on one's emotional health. In hindsight, 2021 was a big year for black female athletes to declare that it was acceptable to not be okay, with Osaka leading the charge. These black female athletes are not afraid to prioritize self-care and take a break!

I believe that self-care is a fundamental human right because it is the only path to self-realization. I also acknowledge that self-realization (to become our best, most fulfilled, and most loving selves) is our ultimate goal as human beings. Self-care yields self-love, which in turn yields self-realization. That sounds refreshing, doesn't it?

I believe that the deliberate act to continue creating more emotional, spiritual, social, financial, and political freedom for black women will ultimately transform the world we have historically carried on our shoulders. To achieve this, we must embrace self-love by practicing self-care. We must also release ourselves from the "I can do it alone" mindset and move toward self-care born of love, sisterhood, and fuller participation in the human family.

Fortunately, you don't need any miracle to start your self-care journey. Just grab a pen and journal and practice the activities highlighted in this book, and you are good to go. Meanwhile, I would love to hear your feedback on your self-care journey and what's working for you. So feel free to share your opinion because doing so can benefit other black women who are struggling with their self-esteem, confidence, relationships, and health.

To your success,

House of Abundance Publications

BIBLIOGRAPHY

FBI:UCR. (2018). 2018 crime in the United States. https://ucr.fbi.gov/crime-in-the-u.s/2018/crime-in-the-u.s.-2018/tables/table-43.

Bhandari, S. (2020). What does stress do to the body? https://www.webmd.com/balance/stress-management/stress-and-the-body.

Cooks-Campbell, A. (2022). How inner child work enables healing and playful discovery. https://www.betterup.com/blog/inner-child-work.

Dutes, K. & Nguyen, A. (2021). Procrastination is more than putting things off. Here's how to kick the habit. https://www.npr.org/2021/01/11/955692434/procrastination-is-more-than-putting-things-off.

Fagan, A. (2018). 30 types of self-sabotage (and what to do about it). https://www.psychologytoday.com/us/blog/in-practice/201805/30-types-self-sabotage-and-what-do-about-it.

Fisher, L. (2014). Shonda Rhimes speaks her mind on 'angry black woman' flap. https://abcnews.go.com/blogs/entertainment/2014/10/shonda-rhimes-speaks-her-mind-on-angry-black-woman-flap.

Geronimus, A. T., Margaret, T. H., Pearson, A. J., Seashols J. S., Brown, Kelly L. B., & Cruz, T. D. (2010). Do US black women experience stress-related accelerated biological aging? https://philpapers.org/rec/GERDUB.

Gupta, S. (2021). We decode the science behind affirmations and how they can infuse positivity in your life. https://www.healthshots.com/mind/happiness-hacks/we-decode-the-science-behind-affirmations-and-how-they-can-infuse-positivity-in-your-life.

HealthCoachInstitute. (2021). 7 Types of Self-Care & Why You Need Them. https://www.healthcoachinstitute.com/articles/7-types-of-self-care.

Jegtvig, S. (2014). African American women have a harder time losing weight. https://www.reuters.com/article/us-african-american-women-weight-idUSBREA020TH20140103.

Pifer, R. (2022). Black women disproportionately concentrated in low-wage, hazardous healthcare jobs, study finds. https://www.healthcaredive.com/news/black-women-disproportionately-concentrated-low-wage-hazardous-health-jobs/618471.

Kindling Zing. (2021). Questions to ask your inner child: childhood regained.

https://kindlingzing.com/questions-to-ask-your-inner-child-childhood-regained.

Kuntz. L. (2020). Are women more frequently diagnosed with anxiety and depression? https://www.psychiatrictimes.com/view/are-women-more-frequently-diagnosed-with-anxiety-and-depression.

MacCutcheon, M. (2019). Weighed down by feelings of guilt and shame? Here's how to overcome them. https://www.goodtherapy.org/blog/weighed-down-by-feelings-of-guilt-shame-how-to-overcome-them-0612194

Martin, K. I. & Redmond, N. (2021). Health equity among black women in the United States. https://www.liebertpub.com/doi/10.1089/jwh.2020.8868.

Moore, C. (2020). 72 mental health questions for counselors and patients. https://positivepsychology.com/mental-health-questions/#examples.

Muorah, C. (2020). What Is racial trauma and how to practice radical self-care. https://councilforrelationships.org/racial-trauma-mind-body-connection-treatment-recovery-wellness.

Raina, S. (2021). Four brain science habits to help neutralize negative self-talk. https://www.forbes.com/sites/forbescoachescouncil/2021/05/06/four-brain-science-habits-to-help-neutralize-negative-self-talk/?sh=161f7ba34f3c.

Spike, C. (2021). 20+ inspiring black women who are breaking barriers and making History. https://www.prevention.com/life/g35452080/famous-black-women.

Samuels, R. (2021). The private grief of Courteney Ross, George Floyd's girl-friend. https://www.washingtonpost.com/nation/interactive/2021/george-floyd-girlfriend-courteney-ross.

Williams, K (2021). The powerful must-have list of positive affirmations for black women. https://kbinbloom.com/positive-affirmations-for-black-women.

Wilson, D. R. (2020). 40 ways to relax in 5 minutes or less. https://greatist.com/happiness/40-ways-relax-5-minutes-or-less.

www.ingramcontent.com/pod-product-compliance
Lightning Source LLC
Chambersburg PA
CBHW071151120626
46546CB00006B/2213